Elements of Language

First
Course

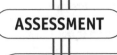
ASSESSMENT

# Assessment Alternatives

**Holistic Scoring: Prompts and Models**

**Rubrics for**
- writing assignments
- optional projects
- oral and visual literacy projects and performances

**Portfolio Management**

**Inventory Forms**

**Evaluation Forms**

**HOLT, RINEHART AND WINSTON**

A Harcourt Classroom Education Company

Austin · New York · Orlando · Atlanta · San Francisco · Boston · Dallas · Toronto · London

## STAFF CREDITS

### EDITORIAL

**Director**
Mescal Evler

**Manager of Editorial Operations**
Bill Wahlgren

**Executive Editor**
Emily Shenk

**Project Editor**
Megan Truex

**Prototyping Editor**
Cheryl Christian

**Contributing Editors**
Jane Archer Feinstein, Ann Michelle Gibson, Sean W. Henry, Errol Smith, Tressa Sanders

**Copyediting**
Michael Neibergall, *Copyediting Manager;* Mary Malone, *Senior Copyeditor;* Joel Bourgeois, Elizabeth Dickson, Gabrielle Field, Jane Kominek, Millicent Ondras, Theresa Reding,

Kathleen Scheiner, Laurie Schlesinger, *Copyeditors*

**Project Administration**
Marie Price, *Managing Editor;* Lori De La Garza, *Editorial Operations Coordinator;* Thomas Browne, Heather Cheyne, Diane Hardin, Mark Holland, Marcus Johnson, Jill O'Neal, Joyce Rector, Janet Riley, Kelly Tankersley, *Project Administration;* Gail Coupland, Ruth Hooker, Margaret Sanchez, *Word Processing*

**Editorial Permissions**
Janet Harrington, *Permissions Editor*

**Writers of Exemplary Student Essays**
Zachary Doll, Lee Guerrero, Shannon Sharp

### ART, DESIGN AND PHOTO

**Graphic Services**
Kristen Darby, *Manager*

**Image Acquisitions**
Joe London, *Director;* Tim Taylor, *Photo Research Supervisor;* Rick Benavides, *Assistant Photo Researcher;* Elaine Tate, *Supervisor;* Erin Cone, *Art Buyer*

**Cover Design**
Sunday Patterson

### PRODUCTION

Belinda Barbosa Lopez, *Senior Production Coordinator*
Simira Davis, *Supervisor*
Nancy Hargis, *Media Production Supervisor*
Joan Lindsay, *Production Coordinator*
Beth Prevelige, *Prepress Manager*

### MANUFACTURING

Michael Roche, *Supervisor of Inventory and Manufacturing*

**Dr. Roger Farr,** author of the essay that appears on pages 1–23, is currently Chancellor's Professor of Education and Director of the Center for Innovation and Assessment at Indiana University. He is a past president of the International Reading Association and the author of both norm-referenced tests and performance assessments. Dr. Farr has taught at both elementary and high school levels in New York State and has served as a school district reading consultant.

The International Reading Association presented Dr. Farr the William S. Gray award for outstanding lifetime contributions to the teaching of reading in 1984. He was elected to the IRA for outstanding lifetime contributions to the teaching of reading in 1984. He was elected to the IRA Reading Hall of Fame in 1986 and was selected by the IRA as the Outstanding Teacher Educator in Reading in 1988.

Printed in the United States of America

ISBN 0-03-057573-7

12345 179 04 03 02 01 00

# Table of Contents

**About This Book** ...........................................................................................................viii

## Portfolio Management

**Introduction to Portfolio Assessment in the Language Arts Classroom**.......1–23

Forms for evaluating and organizing portfolio work

*Forms for the student:*

Summary of My Progress: Writing, Speaking, and Representing ........................................24

Summary of My Progress: Reading, Listening, and Viewing.............................................26

Self-Evaluation: Any Project ........................................................................................28

Peer Evaluation: Any Project ........................................................................................29

My Self-Assessment Record...........................................................................................30

Goal-Setting for Reading, Writing, Speaking, Listening,
Viewing, or Representing...............................................................................................31

Student-Teacher Conference Notes...............................................................................33

Table of Contents: How My Portfolio Is Organized.......................................................34

About My Portfolio ......................................................................................................35

Forms for communication with parents and guardians and for assessing student language use

*Forms for the teacher:*

The Portfolio: What Does It Show? ...............................................................................37

Response to the Portfolio...............................................................................................38

Student Awareness of Language as Process.....................................................................39

Student Performance Graph ..........................................................................................40

## Inventories and Evaluation Forms

**Reading Forms**

*Forms for the student:*

Peer and self-assessment forms for recording student reading, establishing baselines, and setting goals

My Reading Record ......................................................................................................41

Inventory: Some Facts About My Reading....................................................................42

Inventory: Some Facts About My Reading Skills ..........................................................43

Evaluation of My Reading Skills and Strategies: Narration/Description .....................44

Evaluation of My Reading Skills and Strategies: Exposition .......................................46

# Table of Contents

Evaluation of My Reading Skills and Strategies: Persuasion ........................................... 48

Inventory: Some Facts About My Study Skills ................................................................. 50

***Forms for the teacher:***

Progress in Reading ....................................................................................................... 52

Progress in Reading Skills ............................................................................................... 54

Forms for tracking student improvement in reading

## Writing Forms

***Forms for the student:***

Record of My Writing ...................................................................................................... 57

My Spelling Log ............................................................................................................... 58

My Vocabulary Log .......................................................................................................... 59

Inventory: Some Facts About My Writing ........................................................................ 60

Evaluating Your Writing Process ..................................................................................... 61

Assessing Your Writing Process: Analytic Scale .............................................................. 63

Evaluating and Revising Your Draft ................................................................................. 64

Checklist: Evaluating and Revising Your Draft ................................................................ 67

Evaluating Your Content and Organization ..................................................................... 68

Evaluating Your Audience and Purpose ........................................................................... 69

Revising: Your Response as a Reader ............................................................................... 70

Four-Point Analytic Scale for Revising ............................................................................ 71

General Analytic Scale ..................................................................................................... 72

Four-Point Analytic Scale: General .................................................................................. 73

Open Analytic Scale ........................................................................................................ 74

Analytic Scale for Chapter 1: An Eyewitness Account .................................................... 75

Analytic Scale for Chapter 2: Instructions ...................................................................... 76

Analytic Scale for Chapter 3: An Advantages/Disadvantages Essay ............................... 77

Analytic Scale for Chapter 4: A Jacket for a Novel ......................................................... 78

Analytic Scale for Chapter 5: A Report of Information .................................................... 79

Analytic Scale for Chapter 6: A Persuasive Essay ........................................................... 80

Analytic Scale for Chapter 7: A Print Advertisement ...................................................... 81

Proofreading Review ....................................................................................................... 82

Proofreading Checklist .................................................................................................... 83

My Record of Proofreading Corrections .......................................................................... 84

My Multiple-Assignment Proofreading Record ............................................................... 85

Peer and self-assessment forms for recording student writing, establishing baselines, and setting goals

# Table of Contents

My Self-Assessment Record..................................................................86

Evaluating Presentation and Format...................................................87

Forms for tracking student improvement in writing

**Forms for the teacher:**

Progress in Writing................................................................................88

Progress in Writing Conventions........................................................90

Creating a Guide for Evaluating Papers .............................................91

**Speaking and Listening Forms**

**Forms for the student:**

My Speaking and Listening Record .....................................................92

Inventory: Some Facts About My Speaking .......................................93

Inventory: Some Facts About My Listening........................................94

Evaluating My Critical Listening .........................................................95

My Evaluation Checklist for a Speech ................................................97

My Evaluation of a Speech...................................................................98

Evaluating My Oral Presentation of a Literary Text ..........................99

My Evaluation of an Oral Presentation of a Literary Text...............100

My Evaluation of Informative Oral Presentations...........................101

My Evaluation of Persuasive Oral Presentations.............................102

My Evaluation of Oral Storytelling ...................................................103

My Evaluation of a Panel Discussion.................................................104

My Evaluation of a Group Discussion................................................105

Peer and self-assessment forms for recording student speaking and listening activities, establishing baselines, and setting goals

Forms for tracking student improvement in speaking and listening

**Forms for the teacher:**

Progress in Speaking...........................................................................106

Progress in Listening ..........................................................................107

Progress in Oral Presentation of Literary Texts...............................108

Progress in Evaluation of Oral Presentations of Literary Texts ......109

Progress in Evaluating Oral Presentations of Informative and
Persuasive Messages..........................................................................110

Progress in Evaluating Oral Storytelling...........................................111

Progress in Evaluating Panel Discussions .........................................112

Progress in Evaluating Group Discussions ........................................113

# Table of Contents

Peer and self-assessment forms for recording student viewing and representing activities, establishing baselines, and setting goals

**Viewing and Representing Forms**

*Forms for the student:*

My Viewing Record ............................................................................114

Inventory: Some Questions and Answers About My Viewing...................115

Inventory: Some Questions and Answers About My Representing............116

My Evaluation of Multimedia Presentations.........................................117

My Evaluation of a Documentary.........................................................118

My Evaluation of a Newspaper............................................................119

My Evaluation of a Photograph ...........................................................120

My Evaluation of a Television News Program .......................................121

My Comparison of Media: Film and Literature .....................................122

My Evaluation of a Television Entertainment Program .........................123

My Evaluation of Graphics..................................................................124

My Evaluation of a Television Commercial............................................125

My Evaluation of a Print Advertisement...............................................126

My Evaluation of a Web Site ...............................................................127

Forms for tracking student improvement in viewing and representing

*Forms for the teacher:*

Progress in Viewing ...........................................................................128

Progress in Representing ....................................................................129

Progress in Evaluating Multimedia Presentations ................................130

Progress in Evaluating Documentaries.................................................131

Progress in Evaluating Newspapers .....................................................132

Progress in Evaluating Photographs.....................................................133

Progress in Evaluating Television News.................................................134

Progress in Evaluating Film and TV Entertainment Genres....................135

Progress in Evaluating Graphics..........................................................136

Progress in Evaluating Advertising ......................................................137

Progress in Evaluating Web Sites.........................................................138

Peer and self-assessment forms for recording student cooperative learning activities, establishing baselines, and setting goals

**Cooperative Learning Forms**

*Forms for the student:*

My Cooperative Learning Record.........................................................139

Inventory: Some Questions and Answers About My Cooperative Learning ...........140

Evaluation of My Cooperative Learning ...............................................141

# Table of Contents

My Evaluation of Cooperative Learning ...................................................................142

My Evaluation of Group Participation .....................................................................143

Form for tracking student improvement in cooperative learning

***Forms for the teacher:***

Progress in Cooperative Learning .............................................................................144

## Writing Assessment

Rubrics for evaluating on-demand writing with examples and evaluations of student work

**Assessment Rubrics**

Holistic Scale—Six Points: Expository Writing ........................................................145

Holistic Scale—Six Points: Persuasive Writing ........................................................147

Holistic Scale—Six Points: Recommendation of a Book .......................................149

Holistic Scale—Four Points: Expository Writing .....................................................151

Holistic Scale—Four Points: Persuasive Writing .....................................................153

Holistic Scale—Four Points: Recommendation of a Book.....................................155

Six Trait Analytic Scale ............................................................................................157

**Essays and Evaluations: Expository Writing**...............................................163–169

**Essays and Evaluations: Persuasive Writing** .............................................170–176

**Essays and Evaluations: Recommendation of a Book**...............................177–184

## Evaluation Rubrics

Criteria for evaluating the Speaking and Listening and Viewing and Representing *Focus On* Workshops

**Rubrics for Speaking and Listening/Viewing and Representing**

Examining News .......................................................................................................185

Following Oral Instructions .....................................................................................186

Making a Documentary Video..................................................................................187

Designing and Creating a Book Cover.....................................................................188

Performing a Dramatic Reading ..............................................................................189

Giving and Listening to an Informative Speech .....................................................190

Interpreting Graphics and Web Sites.......................................................................191

Analyzing an Editorial Cartoon................................................................................192

Analyzing Visual Effects in Ads ..............................................................................193

Criteria for evaluating the Choices activities presented at the end of every pupil's edition chapter

**Rubrics for *Choices* Activities**

Introduction through Chapter 7................................................................................194–207

# About This Book

This booklet, *Assessment Alternatives,* accompanies the *Elements of Language* series and provides assessment resources for portfolio work, essays written in testing situations, and a variety of classroom activities.

**Part I** | **Portfolio Management**

This section begins with an essay designed to provide an introduction to portfolio work, including suggestions about how to develop and use portfolios and how to conduct conferences with students about their work.

The introductory essay is followed by a set of student forms for assessing and organizing portfolio contents and for setting goals for future work. Also included is a set of teacher forms for communicating with parents or guardians about student work and for generally assessing students' progress.

**Part II** | **Inventories and Evaluation Forms**

These forms can be used to record work, to establish baselines and goals, and to think critically about student work in a variety of areas. These areas include:

- **Reading**
- **Speaking and Listening**
- **Cooperative Learning**
- **Writing**
- **Viewing and Representing**

The goal of these forms is to encourage students to develop criteria for assessing their work and to identify areas for improvement. Many forms can also be used for assessment of a peer's work.

A set of forms for the teacher to use in assessing student progress can be found after the set of student forms for each content area.

**Part III** | **Writing Assessment**

This section contains three different kinds of rubrics for assessing on-demand writing: *Six Point Scales, Four Point Scales,* and *Six Trait Scales.* Accompanying these scales are high-level, mid-level, and low-level examples of student writing. Individual evaluations, based on each of the three rubrics, follow each student essay.

**Part IV** | **Evaluation Rubrics**

Included in this section are sets of criteria for evaluating all *Focus On* workshops and *Choices* activities included in the pupil's edition. These rubrics may be used by students for peer or self-assessment or by the teacher for assessing student work.

# Portfolio Assessment in the Language Arts

Although establishing and using a portfolio assessment system requires a certain amount of time, effort, and understanding, an increasing number of teachers believe that the benefits of implementing such a system richly reward their efforts.

Language arts portfolios are collections of materials that display aspects of students' use of language. They are a means by which students can collect samples of their written work over time so that they and their teachers can ascertain how the students are developing as language users. Because reflection and self-assessment are built-in aspects of language arts portfolios, both also help students develop their critical-thinking and metacognitive abilities.

Each portfolio collection is typically kept in a folder, box, or other container to which items are added on a regular basis. The collection can include a great variety of materials, depending on the design of the portfolio assessment program, the kinds of projects completed inside and outside of the classroom, and the interests of individual students. For example, portfolios may contain student stories, essays, sketches, poems, letters, journals, and other original writing, and they may also contain reactions to articles, stories, and other texts the student has read. Other materials that are suitable for inclusion in portfolios are drawings, photographs, audiotapes, and videotapes of students taking part in special activities; clippings and pictures from newspapers and magazines; and notes on favorite authors and on stories and books that the student hopes to read. Many portfolios also include several versions of the same piece of writing, demonstrating how the writing has developed through revision.

Finally, portfolios may contain logs of things the student has read or written, written reflections or assessments of portfolio work, and tables and explanations about the way the portfolio is organized. (A collection of forms that can be used to generate these items may be found on page 24 following this essay and in Part II of this booklet.)

## The Advantages of Portfolio Assessment

How can portfolio assessment help you meet your instructional goals? Here are some of the most important advantages of using portfolios:

- *Portfolios link instruction and assessment.* Traditional testing is usually one or more steps removed from the process or performance being assessed. However, because portfolio assessment focuses on performance—on students' actual use of language—portfolios are a highly accurate gauge of what students have learned in the classroom.

- *Portfolios involve students in assessing their own language use and abilities.* Portfolio assessment can provide some of the most effective learning opportunities available in your classroom. In fact, the assessment is itself instructional: Students, as self-assessors, identify their own strengths and weaknesses. Furthermore, portfolios are a natural way to develop metacognition in your students. As the collected work is analyzed, the student begins to think critically about how he or she makes meaning while reading, writing, speaking, and listening. For example, the student begins to ask questions while reading, such as "Is this telling me what I need to know?" "Am I enjoying this author as much as I expected to?" "Why or why not?" While writing, the student may ask, "Am I thinking about the goals I set when I was analyzing my portfolio?" That's what good instruction is all about: getting students to use the skills you help them develop.

- *Portfolios invite attention to important aspects of language.* Because most portfolios include numerous writing samples, they naturally direct attention to diction, style, main idea or theme, author's purpose, and other aspects of language that are difficult to assess in other ways. The portfolio encourages awareness and appreciation of these aspects of language as they occur in literature and nonfiction as well as in the student's own work.

- *Portfolios emphasize language use as a process that integrates language behaviors.* Students who keep and analyze portfolios develop an understanding that reading, writing, speaking, listening, viewing, and representing are all aspects of a larger process. They come to see that language behaviors are connected by thinking about and expressing one's own ideas and feelings.

- *Portfolios make students aware of audience and the need for a writing purpose.* Students develop audience awareness by regularly analyzing their portfolio writing samples. Evaluation forms prompt them to reflect on whether they have defined and appropriately addressed their audience. Moreover, because portfolios provide or support opportunities for students to work together, peers can often provide feedback about how well a student has addressed an audience in his or her work. Finally, students may be asked to consider particular audiences (parents, classmates, or community groups, for example) who will review their portfolios; they may prepare explanations of the contents for such audiences, and they may select specific papers to present as a special collection to such audiences.

- *Portfolios provide a vehicle for student interaction and cooperative learning.* Many projects that normally involve cooperative learning produce material for portfolios. Portfolios, in turn, provide or support many opportunities for students to work together. Students

As they become attuned to audience, students automatically begin to be more focused on whether their work has fulfilled their purpose for writing. They begin to ask: "Did I say what I meant to say? Could I have been clearer and more effective? Do I understand what this writer wants to tell me? Do I agree with it?" Speaking and listening activities can also be evaluated in terms of audience awareness and clarity of purpose.

# Portfolio Assessment in the Language Arts *(continued)*

can work as partners or as team members who critique each other's collections. For example, students might work together to prepare, show, and explain portfolios to particular audiences, such as parents, administrators, and other groups interested in educational progress and accountability.

- *Portfolios can incorporate many types of student expression on a variety of topics.* Students should be encouraged to include materials from different subject areas and from outside school, especially materials related to hobbies and other special interests. In this way, students come to see language arts skills as crucial tools for authentic, real-world work.

- *Portfolios provide genuine opportunities to learn about students and their progress as language users.* Portfolio contents can reveal to the teacher a great deal about the student's background and interests with respect to reading, writing, speaking, listening, viewing, and representing. Portfolios can also demonstrate the student's development as a language user and reveal areas where he or she needs improvement.

# How to Develop and Use Portfolios

As you begin designing a portfolio program for your students, you may wish to read articles and reports that discuss the advantages of portfolio assessment. The reading list on page 23 can help you get started.

## Basic Design Features

For a portfolio program to be successful in the classroom, the program should reflect the teacher's particular instructional goals and the students' needs as learners. Teachers are encouraged to customize a portfolio program for their classrooms, although most successful portfolio programs share a core of essential portfolio management techniques. Following are suggestions that teachers will want to consider in customizing a portfolio program.

- *Integrate portfolio assessment into the regular classroom routine.* Teachers should make portfolio work a regular class activity by providing opportunities for students to work with their collections during class time. During these portfolio sessions, the teacher should promote analysis (assessment) that reflects his or her instructional objectives and goals.

- *Link the program to classroom activities.* Student portfolios should contain numerous examples of classroom activities and projects. To ensure that portfolios reflect the scope of students' work, some teachers require that certain papers and assignments be included.

You may want to require that certain papers, projects, and reports be included in the portfolio. Such requirements should be kept to a minimum so that students feel that they can include whatever they consider to be relevant to their language development.

- *Let students have the control.* Students can develop both self-assessment and metacognition skills when they select and arrange portfolio contents themselves. This practice also develops a strong sense of ownership: students feel that their portfolios belong to them, not to the teacher. When students take ownership of their work, they accept more responsibility for their own language development. To encourage a sense of ownership on the part of students, portfolios should be stored where students can get at them easily, and students should have regular and frequent access to their portfolios.

- *Include students' creative efforts.* To ensure that the portfolios develop a range of language skills, encourage students to include samples of their creative writing, pieces they have written outside of class, and publishing activities that they may have participated in, such as the production of a class magazine.

Portfolios that include such planning papers and intermediate drafts are called *working portfolios.* Working portfolios force the student to organize and analyze the material collected, an activity that makes clear to the student that language use is process.

- *Make sure portfolios record students' writing process.* If portfolios are to teach language use as a process that integrates various language behaviors, they need to contain papers that show how writing grows out of planning and develops through revision. Portfolios should include notes, outlines, clippings, reactions to reading or oral presentations, pictures, and other materials that inspired the final product. Equally vital to the

# How to Develop and Use Portfolios *(continued)*

The act of selecting particular papers to show to special audiences—parents, another teacher, or the principal, to name a few—refines students' sense of audience. Preparing and presenting selected collections, called *show portfolios*, engages students in a more sophisticated analysis of their work and encourages them to visualize the audience for the show collection.

If students feel free to include writing and reading done outside of class in their portfolios, you can discover interests, opinions, and concerns that can be touched on during conferences. In turn, by communicating interest in and respect for what engages the student, you can promote the success of the portfolio program.

portfolio collections are the different drafts of papers that demonstrate revision over a period of time. Such collections can promote fruitful, concrete discussions between student and teacher about how the student's process shaped the final product.

- *Rely on reactions to reading and listening.* If portfolios are to link and interrelate language behaviors, students must be encouraged to include reactions to things they read and hear. During conferences, teachers may want to point out how some of the student's work has grown out of listening or reading.

- *Encourage students to consider the audience.* Portfolio building prompts students to think about the audience because, as a kind of publication, the portfolio invites a variety of readers. Students will become interested in and sensitive to the reactions of their classmates and their teacher, as well as to the impact of the collections on any other audiences that may be allowed to view them.

- *Promote collaborative products.* Portfolios can promote student collaboration if the program sets aside class time for students to react to one another's work and to work in groups. This interaction can occur informally or in more structured student partnerships or team responses. In addition, many writing projects can be done by teams and small groups, and any common product can be reproduced for all participants' portfolios. Performance projects, speeches, and other oral presentations often require cooperative participation. Audiotapes and videotapes of collaborative projects may be included in portfolios.

- *Let the portfolios reflect a variety of subject areas and interests.* The language arts portfolio should include material from subject areas other than language arts. Broadening the portfolio beyond the language arts classroom is important if the student is to understand that reading, writing, speaking, and listening are authentic activities—that is, that they are central to all real-world activities. Any extensive attempt to limit portfolio contents may suggest to students that reading and writing skills relate only to the language arts classroom.

## Initial Design Considerations

Using what you have read so far, you can make some initial notes as guidelines for drafting your portfolio assessment design. You can complete a chart like the one on the next page to plan how you will use portfolios and what you can do to make them effective.

# How to Develop and Use Portfolios *(continued)*

| What are my primary goals in developing my students' ability to use language? | How can portfolios contribute to meeting these goals? | What design features can ensure this? |
|---|---|---|
| | | |
| | | |
| | | |
| | | |
| | | |
| | | |

# How to Develop and Use Portfolios *(continued)*

Some key considerations for designing a portfolio program have been suggested above. Other considerations will arise as you assess ways to use the portfolios. Here are some questions that will probably arise in the planning stages of portfolio assessment.

**How can** I introduce students to the concepts of portfolio management?

**What examples** of student work should go into the portfolios?

**What should** the criteria be for deciding what will be included?

**How and** where will the portfolio collections be kept?

## Designing a Portfolio Program

### How can I introduce students to the concepts of portfolio management?

One way is to experiment with a group of your students. If you use this limited approach, be sure to select students with varied reading and writing abilities to get a sense of how portfolios work for students with a range of skill levels. To introduce portfolio assessment to them, you can either talk to students individually or as a group about what they will be doing. If other students begin expressing an interest in keeping portfolios, let them take part as well. The kind of excitement that builds around portfolio keeping almost guarantees that some students not included initially will want to get on board for the trial run; some may start keeping portfolios on their own.

You might let students help you design or at least plan some details of the system. After explaining both the reasons for keeping portfolios and the elements of the program that you have decided are essential, you can let students discuss how they think certain aspects should be handled. Even if you decide you want students to make important decisions concerning the program's design, you will need to have a clear idea of what your teaching objectives are and of what you will ask students to do.

### What examples of student work should go into the portfolios?

Portfolios should reflect as much as possible the spectrum of your students' language use. What you want to ensure is that student self-assessment leads to the understanding that language skills are essential to all learning. For this to happen, portfolios should contain reading, writing, speaking, listening, viewing, and representing activities that relate to a number of subject areas and interests, not just to the language arts. Moreover, the portfolio should include final, completed works as well as drafts, notes, freewriting, and other samples that show the student's thinking and writing process.

**FINAL PRODUCTS** Students should consider including pieces that are created with a general audience in mind; writing that is communicative and intended for particular audiences; and writing that is very personal and that is used as a method of thinking through situations, evaluating experiences, or musing simply for enjoyment. The portfolios can contain a variety of finished products, including

- original stories, dialogue, and scripts
- poems

# How to Develop and Use Portfolios *(continued)*

- essays, themes, sketches
- song lyrics
- original videos
- video or audio recordings of performances
- narrative accounts of experiences
- correspondence with family members and friends
- stream-of-consciousness pieces
- journals of various types

Examples of various types of journals that students might enjoy keeping are described below.

## Keeping Journals

A journal is an excellent addition to a portfolio—and one that teachers report is very successful. Journal keeping develops the habit of recording one's observations, feelings, and ideas. At the same time, journal writing is an excellent way to develop fluency. Specifically, it can help tentative writers to overcome the reluctance to put thoughts down as words. Journal keeping can be a bridge over inhibitions to writing and can become a student's favorite example of his or her language use. All this recommends the addition of journals to the portfolio.

The success with journals in encouraging young writers has led teachers to experiment with a variety of types:

**PERSONAL JOURNAL** This form of journal allows the writer to make frequent entries (regularly or somewhat irregularly) on any topic and for any purpose. This popular and satisfying kind of journal writing develops writing fluency and reveals to students the essential relationship between thinking and writing. (If the journal is kept in the portfolio, you may wish to remind students that you will be viewing it. Tell students to omit anything they would not be comfortable sharing.)

**LITERARY JOURNAL OR READER'S LOG** This journal provides a way of promoting open-ended and freewheeling responses to student reading. Students are usually allowed to structure and organize these journals in any way that satisfies them. As a collection of written responses, the literary journal is a valuable source of notes for oral and written expression; it can also give students ideas for further reading. Finally, the literary journal is another tool that reveals to students that reading, writing, and thinking are interrelated.

**TOPICAL JOURNAL** This style of journal is dedicated to a particular interest or topic. It is a valuable experience for students to be allowed to express themselves freely about a specific topic—a favorite hobby, pastime, or issue, for example.

# How to Develop and Use Portfolios *(continued)*

As with the literary journal, the topical journal can point students toward project ideas and further reading.

**DIALOGUE JOURNAL** For this journal format, students select one person—a classmate, friend, family member, or teacher, for example—to strike up a continuing dialogue with. Dialogue journals help develop audience awareness and can promote cooperative learning. If students in your class are keeping dialogue journals with each other, be prepared to help them decide in whose portfolio the journal will go. (Because making copies may be too time consuming or expensive, you could help students arrange alternate custody, or have them experiment by keeping two distinct journals.)

## Fragments and Works in Progress

In addition to finished products, portfolios should include papers showing how your students are processing ideas as readers, writers, speakers, and listeners. Drafts that show how writing ideas are developed through revision are especially helpful as students assess their work. Items that demonstrate how your language users are working with their collections can include

- articles, news briefs, sketches, or other sources collected and used as the basis for written or oral projects. These "seeds" may include pictures created or collected by students and used for inspiration for the subject. The portfolio may also include some items that have not yet been developed.
- reading-response notes that have figured in the planning of a paper and have been incorporated into the final work. Once again, some notes may be intended for future projects.
- other notes, outlines, or evidence of planning for papers written or ready to be drafted
- pieces in which the student is thinking out a problem or considering a topic of interest or behavior or is planning something for the future. These pieces may include pro and con arguments, and persuasive points and reactions to reading.
- freewriting, done either at school or at home
- early versions (drafts) of the latest revision of a piece of writing
- notes analyzing the student's latest draft, which may direct subsequent revision
- solicited reactions from classmates or the teacher
- a published piece accompanied by revised manuscripts showing edits

# How to Develop and Use Portfolios *(continued)*

- correspondence from relatives and friends to which students have written a response or to which students need to respond
- journal or diary entries that are equivalent to preliminary notes or drafts of a piece of writing
- tapes of conversations or interviews to which a piece of writing refers or on which it is based

While test results in general do not make good contents for portfolios, performance assessments can provide a focused example of both language processing and integration of reading and writing skills. Such performance tests are now frequently structured as realistic tasks that require reading, synthesizing, and reacting to particular texts. More often than not, these assessments guide the student through planning stages and a preliminary draft. (These parts of the assessment are rarely rated, but they lend themselves directly to self-analysis and should definitely be included with the final draft.)

### What should the criteria be for deciding what will be included?

Teachers often want to ensure that students keep certain kinds of papers in the portfolios, while also affirming students' need for a genuine sense of ownership of their collections. Achieving a balance between these two general objectives may not be as difficult as it seems. Students can be informed at the time that they are introduced to the portfolio concept that they will be asked to keep certain items as one part of the overall project. Almost certainly, it will be necessary to explain at some point that the collections are to be working portfolios and that certain records—including many of the forms provided in this booklet—will also need to be included. As they become accustomed to analyzing the papers in their portfolios, students can be encouraged or required to select the contents of their portfolios, using criteria that they develop themselves. Teachers can help students articulate these criteria in informal and formal conferences. Following are criteria teachers or students might consider:

- papers that students think are well done and that therefore represent their best efforts, or papers that were difficult to complete
- subjects that students enjoyed writing about, or texts they have enjoyed reading; things that they think are interesting or will interest others
- things that relate to reading or writing students intend to do in the future, including ideas that may be developed into persuasive essays, details to support positions on issues, and reaction to favorite literary texts

Discourage the inclusion of workbook sheets, unless they contain ideas for future student writing; they tend to obscure the message that language development is a process, a major component of which is the expression of student ideas and opinions.

You might want to brainstorm a list of things that could be kept in your students' portfolios and then prioritize the items on your list according to which ones you think will be essential for students' development.

# How to Develop and Use Portfolios (continued)

- papers that contain ideas or procedures that students wish to remember

- incomplete essays or projects that presented some problem for the student. He or she may plan to ask a parent, teacher, or fellow student to react to the work or to earlier drafts.

- work that students would like particular viewers of the portfolio (the teacher, their parents, their classmates, and so on) to see, for some reason. This criterion is one that will dictate selections for a show portfolio; it may also determine some of the papers selected for the overall collection.

After building their collections for some time, students should be able to examine them and make lists of their selection criteria in their own words. Doing so should balance out any requirements the teacher has set for inclusion and should ensure students' sense of ownership.

A final note on selection criteria for student portfolios: While portfolios should certainly contain students' best efforts, too often teachers and students elect to collect only their "best stuff." An overemphasis on possible audiences that might view the collection can make it seem important that the collection be a show portfolio. Preparing show portfolios for particular audiences can require students to assess their work in order to decide what is worth including. That is a worthwhile experience, but once the preparation for the show has been completed, student self-assessment ends.

### How and where will the portfolio collections be kept?

Part of the fun of keeping portfolios is deciding what the holders for the collections will look like. In a few classrooms, portfolio holders are standardized, but in most classes, the students are allowed to create their own. Many teachers allow students to furnish their own containers or folders, as long as these are big enough to hold the collections without students' having to fold or roll the papers—and not so large as to create storage problems. In addition, many teachers encourage their students to decorate their portfolio holders in unique, colorful, personal, and whimsical ways. Allowing this individuality creates enthusiasm for the project. It also helps students develop a genuine sense of ownership, an important attitude to foster if this system is to succeed.

The kinds of holders that students are likely to bring to school include household cardboard boxes, stationery boxes, folders of various types, paper or plastic shopping bags, computer paper boxes, and plastic and cardboard containers for storing clothing and other items. It would be a good idea to

Start collecting some samples of holders you can show when you introduce portfolio management to your students. Decorate at least one sample, or have a young friend or relative do it. At the same time, be thinking about areas in your classroom where the collections can be kept.

# How to Develop and Use Portfolios *(continued)*

have several different examples to show students when discussing how they will keep their papers. It is also a good idea to have some holders on hand for students who are unable to find anything at home that they think is suitable, and for use as replacements for unworkable holders some students may bring, such as shoe boxes that are too small to hold the portfolio items.

The resulting storage area will probably not be neatly uniform but will not necessarily be unattractive, either. Teachers who want a tidier storage area might find similar boxes to pass out to all students, who are then allowed to personalize them in different ways.

The amount of space available in a particular classroom will, of course, determine where students keep their collections, but it is vital that the area be accessible to students. It will save a great deal of inconvenience during the school year if the portfolios are on open shelves or on an accessible ledge of some kind and are not too far from students. If students can retrieve and put away their portfolios in less than a minute or two, there will be many instances when portfolio work can be allowed. Deciding where to keep the portfolios is a decision that may be put off until students know enough about the process to help make the decision.

Open access to portfolios does create the possibility of students looking at classmates' collections without permission and without warning. It seems only fair to remind students not to include in their portfolio anything they would not want others to see. A caution from the teacher could save a student from a wounding embarrassment.

# Conferencing with Students

If you are new at conducting portfolio conferences, ask a student who has kept one or more papers to sit down and talk with you. Talk with the student about what he or she thinks is strong about the paper, how it came to be written, and what kind of reading or research the student undertook. See how well you can promote an open-ended conversation related to the topic of the paper and to language use.

You may wish to try out the Student-Teacher Conference Notes worksheet on page 33. After the conference, think about what you could do to ensure a productive portfolio conference that would be helpful and worthwhile to students.

The regular informal exchanges between teacher and student about portfolio content are obviously very important, but the more formal conferences that anchor a successful program are of equal if not greater importance. Conferences are evidence that both the teacher and the student take the portfolio collection seriously and that the usefulness of the portfolio depends on an ongoing analysis of it. By blocking out time to conduct at least four formal conferences with each student each year, the teacher demonstrates a commitment to the program and a genuine interest in each student's progress.

## Conducting Portfolio Conferences

The conference should proceed as a friendly but clearly directed conversation between the student and the teacher. The focus of the conference should be on how the use of language serves the student's needs and interests. This focus translates, in the course of the conference, into helping each student reflect on why and how he or she reads and writes.

Teachers will want to discuss with students the quantity of recent reading and writing compared with that of previous time periods, the kinds of reading and writing that the student has done, and the student's purposes for reading and writing. (Build on discussions about texts and authors by recommending related reading.) Teachers will also want to discuss how the inclusions in the portfolio came to be and whether the pieces represent experiences and ideas the student has enjoyed and thinks are important. Teachers should let students know that the portfolio documents say something important about the individual student's life. In fact, a significant portion of the conference may be dedicated to learning about the student's interests. Here are a few examples of the types of statements that might elicit a helpful response:

- You seem to know a lot about deep-sea diving.
- Where did you learn all those details?
- Have you looked for books about them?
- Why don't you write something about them?

The student, too, should feel free to ask questions:

- Which pieces seem the best to the teacher and why?
- Is it always necessary to write for some audience?
- What if a writer wants an idea or thought to be vague—remain private, though written?
- How can a writer stop to use reference materials to find the right word and spell it correctly without losing the flow of expression?

# Conferencing with Students *(continued)*

These examples show how the conference can provide powerful, effective opportunities to teach and to guide language development. The conference conversations between the teacher and the student should be as unique as the individual student who joins the teacher in this exchange.

Ideally, each student will look forward to the conference as a time when student and teacher pay close attention to what the student has done; how the student feels about that performance; and what the student's needs and goals are. Such conferences encourage students to accept responsibility for their own development.

The following guidelines will help the teacher make the most of portfolio conferences.

## Conference Guidelines

For many teachers, the time and planning that the conference demands constitute the most difficult aspect of portfolio assessment. Think about how you can use all the resources at your disposal, and don't forget to enlist students' help. Ask them to help you schedule meetings, and request their cooperation so that the system functions smoothly.

Questions will undoubtedly occur to you while reviewing the student's portfolio. It may be useful to have a few notes to remind you of things you would like to ask. Do not, however, approach a conference with a list that dictates the exchange with the student.

- *Conferences should be conducted without interruption.* Plan creatively: Perhaps a volunteer assistant can manage the rest of the class during meetings. Or, assign to other students cooperative-learning activities or other work that does not disrupt your exchange with the student. It may be necessary to conduct the conference outside class time.

- *Keep the focus on the student.* Make the conference as much like an informal conversation as possible by asking questions that will emphasize student interests, attitudes toward reading and writing, favorite authors, and topics they enjoy reading about. Demonstrate that you care what the student thinks and likes. You can also show that you respect the way a student's individuality is manifested in language use.

- *Let the conversation develop naturally.* Be an active listener: Give full attention to what the student is saying. The student's contribution is likely to suggest a question or comment from you, resulting in a genuine and natural exchange. There may be opportunities to get back to questions the teacher had hoped to ask, but teachers should respect the course that the exchange takes and realize that some of their planned questions will need to be dropped. Good listening on the part of the teacher will help create successful conferences that address individual student interests and needs.

- *Be sincere but not judgmental.* Avoid evaluating or passing judgment on interests or aspects of the student's language use. On the other hand, try to avoid continually expressing approval and thereby creating a situation in which the student tries to respond in a way that will win favor: The conference will then lose its focus on the individual's language needs and development.

# Conferencing with Students *(continued)*

Don't hesitate to use the conference as a means of getting to know the student better by learning about his or her interests, pastimes, concerns, and opinions. This can be time well spent, particularly if it demonstrates to the student that the various aspects of his or her life can be very closely connected to the use and development of language arts skills.

Shortly after the conference, the student can translate his or her notes to a worksheet like the goal-setting form on page 31, which will ask the student to elaborate on the objectives that have been established.

- *Keep the conversation open and positive.* It is fine to ask questions that direct the focus back to the collection, as long as that leads in turn to a discussion of ideas and content, the process of reading and writing, and indications of the student's strengths and progress as a language user. In general, however, teachers should ask questions that promise to open up discussion, not shut it down. Phrase questions and comments so that they invite elaboration and explanation.

- *Gear the conference toward goal setting.* Identify and come to an agreement about the goals and objectives the student will be attending to during the next time period.

- *Limit the attention devoted to usage errors.* If the student needs to focus on mechanical or grammatical problems, suggest that over the next time period the student pay particular attention to these problems when editing and revising. Do not, however, turn the session into a catalogue of language errors encountered. Keep in mind that if there are four conferences and each one tactfully encourages a focus on just one or two examples of non-standard mechanical usage, it is possible to eliminate from four to eight high-priority errors during the course of a school year.

- *Keep joint notes with the student on the conference.* To keep a focus on the most important aspects of the conference, you and the student should use the *Student-Teacher Conference Notes* form. Frequently, student and teacher will record notes based on the same observation: For example, the student might write, "I like to use a lot of verbs at the beginning of my sentences, but maybe I use too many." And the teacher might write, "Let's watch to see how often Cody frontshifts sentence elements for emphasis." The student might write, "Look for a novel about the Civil War." The teacher might note, "Find a copy of *The Killer Angels* for Cody if possible." The model for conference notes in this guide allows the two participants to make notes on the same sheet, side by side; thus, notes on the same point will roughly correspond. The teacher and the student can even write at the same time if they can position the note sheet in a way that will facilitate this.

Keep in mind that conference notes frequently serve as a reference point for an action plan that is then more fully considered on the goal-setting worksheet.

## Types of Student-Teacher Conferences

In addition to the scheduled conference, there are several other types of conferences that teachers can conduct as a part of portfolio assessment:

# Conferencing with Students *(continued)*

**GOAL CLARIFICATION CONFERENCES** If a student appears to be having trouble using the portfolio system, a goal clarification conference can be scheduled. The meeting's focus should be to help the student clarify and articulate objectives so that work on the collection is directed and productive.

It is important that this session not be perceived as being overly critical of the student. Be supportive and positive about the collection; try to generate a discussion that will lead to clear goals for the student. These objectives can be articulated on a goal-setting worksheet, which the teacher can help the student fill out.

**PUBLICATION STAFF CONFERENCES** Students who are publishing pieces they write may frequently meet as teams or in staff conferences to select pieces from their portfolio. They may also discuss possible revisions of manuscripts they hope to publish. Teachers may enjoy observing and even participating in these but should let students direct them as much as possible.

Other class projects and collaborative activities can generate similar student conferences that may involve portfolio collections.

**INFORMAL OR ROVING CONFERENCES** In these conferences, teachers consult with students about their portfolios during impromptu sessions. For example, at any time a teacher might encounter a student with an important and intriguing question, or spot confusion or a situation developing into frustration for a self-assessor. Often the situation calls for effective questioning and then good listening, just as in the regularly scheduled conferences.

# Questions and Answers

The questions that follow are frequently asked by teachers who are thinking about instituting a portfolio management system.

- How can I make my students familiar and comfortable with the idea of creating portfolios?
- How often should my students work on their portfolios?
- How can I keep the portfolios from growing too bulky to manage and analyze effectively?
- Should I grade my students' portfolios?
- Who else, besides the student and me, should be allowed to see the portfolio?
- How can I protect against the possible negative effects of allowing a wide variety of persons to see students' portfolios?

### How can I make my students comfortable with portfolios?

Teachers will, of course, want to begin by describing what portfolios are and what they are designed to accomplish. One way to help students visualize portfolios is to point out that some professionals keep portfolios:

- Artists usually keep portfolios to show prospective clients or employers what kind of work they can do. In a sense, an artist's studio is one big working portfolio, full of projects in various stages of completion.
- Photographers, architects, clothing designers, interior designers, and a host of other professionals keep portfolios full of samples of their work.
- Models carry portfolios of pictures showing them in a variety of styles and situations.
- Some writers keep portfolios of their work.
- People who invest their money in stocks and bonds call the collection of different investments they hold a portfolio.

Teachers can encourage students' interest by inviting to the classroom someone who can exhibit and explain a professional portfolio. Teachers might also show students an actual language arts portfolio created by a student in another class or school. Some teachers put together a portfolio of their own and use it as an example for their students.

After this or another introduction, you might share the following information with students:

- Explain what kinds of things will go into the portfolios and why. Students can choose what to include in their collections, but teachers can indicate that a few items will be required, including some records. Without introducing all the records to be used, teachers might show and explain basic forms, such as logs. If forms filled out by students are available, use them as examples.

# Questions and Answers *(continued)*

- Stress that portfolios will be examined regularly. If the working portfolios will be available to parents or others, be sure to inform students. If you plan for others to see only show portfolios, this might be a good time to introduce this kind of portfolio.
- Show examples of holders that might be used, and explain where they will be kept. Students can be involved in making decisions about how and where portfolios will be housed.

### How often should my students work on their portfolios?

The answer is "regularly and often." Teachers should schedule half-hour sessions weekly; ideally, there will be time almost every day when students can work on their collections. The Scheduling Plan on the next page shows activities that should occur regularly in your program.

### How can I keep the portfolios from growing too bulky to manage and analyze effectively?

Because portfolios are intended to demonstrate students' products and processes over time, collections should be culled only when necessary. However, working portfolios can become simply too big, bulky, and clumsy to organize and analyze. If some students find their collections too unwieldy to work with, encourage them to try one of the following techniques:

- Cull older pieces except for those that stand as the best work examples. Put the removed contents into a separate holder and complete an *About My Portfolio* record. Explain on the record that the work consists of less-favored work, and have students take it home for parents to examine and/or save. Photocopies of later work that you consider more successful can be included as comparison.
- Close the whole collection, except for writing not yet completed, notes and records the student intends to use, and other idea files. Send the entire collection home with an explanation record and start a new portfolio.
- Cull from the collection one or more show portfolios for particular audiences, such as parents, other relatives, other teachers, administrators, or supervisors. After the show portfolio has been viewed, return it to the rest of the collection. Start a new portfolio, beginning with the ideas in progress.

Some teachers have their students prepare a larger decorated box to take home at the beginning of the school year. This container eventually holds banded groups of papers culled during the year. Students then have one repository for their entire portfolio collection, which they can keep indefinitely.

# Questions and Answers *(continued)*

## SCHEDULING PLAN FOR PORTFOLIO ASSESSMENT

| Activity | Frequency | The Student | The Teacher |
|---|---|---|---|
| Keeping logs | As reading, writing, and other language experiences are completed; daily if necessary | Makes the entries on the *My Reading Record, My Writing Record, My Speaking and Listening Record,* and My *Viewing Record* | Encourages the student to make regular entries and discusses with the student indications of progress, developing interests, etc. |
| Collecting writing samples, reactions to reading, entries that reflect on oral language | As drafts and reactions to reading become available; can be as often as daily | Selects materials to be included | Can select materials to be included; may require some inclusions |
| Keeping journal(s) | Ongoing basis; daily to at least once a week | Makes regular entries in one or more journals | Analyzes journal writing discreetly and confidentially |
| Adding notes, pictures, clippings, and other idea sources | Weekly or more often | Clips and collects ideas and adds them to appropriate place in the portfolio | Reacts to student's idea sources (every month or so); discusses with student how he or she will use them |
| Explaining, analyzing, evaluating inclusions | Weekly; not less than every other week | Uses forms for evaluating and organizing work to analyze and describe individual pieces included | Analyzes inclusions and student analysis of them at least four times a year—before conferences |
| Completing summary analyses | Monthly and always before conference | Completes a *Summary of Progress* record while comparing it with previously completed summary | Completes selected *Progress Reports* at least four times a year—before conferences, relying on student summaries and previously completed records |
| Conferencing—informal | Ongoing; ideally, at least once a week | Freely asks teacher for advice as often as needed; shares emerging observations with teacher | Makes an effort to observe student working on portfolio at least every two weeks and to discuss one or more specific new inclusions and analyses |
| Conferencing—formal | At least four times a year | Prepares for conference by completing summaries; discusses portfolio contents and analysis of them with teacher; devises new goals; takes joint notes | Prepares for conference with evaluative analyses; discusses portfolio contents and analysis with student; establishes new goals; takes joint notes |
| Preparing explanation of portfolio and analysis of it to a particular audience | As occasion for allowing other audiences access arises | Thoughtfully fills out the form *About My Portfolio* | Keeps student advised as to when other audiences might be looking at the student's collection and who the viewer(s) will be |
| Reacting to a fellow student's paper or portfolio | When it is requested by a "partner" or other classmate | Completes the *Peer Evaluation: Any Project* form | Encourages collaboration whenever possible |

# Questions and Answers *(continued)*

### Should I grade my students' portfolios?

Teachers might be tempted to grade portfolios to let students know that they are accountable for their work; teachers may also feel that a grade legitimizes—or at least recognizes—the time and effort that goes into successful portfolio assessment. Finally, many parents, school supervisors, and administrators will expect the teacher to grade the portfolio. These reasons notwithstanding, most portfolio experts recommend that portfolios not be graded. Keep in mind that the collection will contain papers that have been graded. A grade for the collection as a whole, however, risks undermining the goals of portfolio management. Grading portfolios may encourage students to include only their "best" work, and that practice may convey the message that student self-assessment is not taken seriously. Think about it: How would you feel if someone decided to incorporate your journal entries, your collection of ideas that interest you, and other notes and informal jottings into a package that was being rated and given a grade?

### Who, besides the student and me, should see the portfolio?

This question raises some of the same concerns as the issue of grading portfolios. Teachers may feel some responsibility to let parents, a supervisor, the principal, and fellow faculty members know how the program is proceeding and what it shows about the progress of individuals or of the class as a whole. It is important to balance the benefits of showing portfolios to outside audiences against the possible adverse effects—the risk of inhibiting students, diminishing their sense of ownership, or invading their privacy. Above all, the primary aims of portfolio assessment must be kept in mind.

Following are some suggestions for showing portfolios, with respect to the audience involved.

**PARENTS OR GUARDIANS** Family members will almost certainly be viewing the portfolio in one form or another. If parents or other responsible adults are to view collections only on more formal occasions, such as back-to-school night or during unscheduled visits to the classroom, then students should be assisted in creating show portfolios. If, on the other hand, the teacher will show students' portfolios without the owners' knowledge or chance to review the contents beforehand, the teacher must tell students this at the beginning of the year. Warning students of these unscheduled viewings may qualify their sense of ownership; it can also intensify their audience awareness.

Another way to involve parents in portfolio management is to let students plan a workshop on portfolio management geared for parents and others who are interested. Or, as suggested earlier, have students cull their collections periodically and take the materials home for their parents to see.

# Questions and Answers *(continued)*

Again, if portfolios will be shown to other educators, students should be made aware of this before they start to build their collections.

**SCHOOL SUPERVISORS AND PRINCIPALS** Students' portfolios can demonstrate to fellow educators how youngsters develop as language users, thinkers, and people; they can also show the kind of learning that is taking place in the classroom. When working portfolios are shown, they are usually selected at random from those kept in the class, and the owner's identity is masked. Show portfolios are usually prepared specifically for this purpose. Whether the teacher uses working or show collections (assuming the state or school system does not mandate one) may depend partly on whether she or he thinks the audience will be able to appreciate that the working collections show process.

**CLASSMATES** Students may review their peers' portfolios as part of the program's assessment. Even if a particular program does not include a formal peer review stage, remind students that peers may see their collections—either in the process of collaborative work or peer review, or because a student does not respect the privacy of others.

**NEXT YEAR'S TEACHERS** At the end of the school year, teachers can help students create a show portfolio for their next teacher or teachers. These portfolios should demonstrate the student's growth during the year and the potential of his or her best efforts. They should also indicate the most recent goals established by the teacher and the student, so that the new teacher knows how the student sees his or her language skills developing over the next year.

Encourage students to include finished projects as well as earlier drafts. Discuss what kinds of logs should be included—or have students prepare a brief report showing how goals have been met. A fresh table of contents would be useful, as would an explanation of what the show collection includes and what its purpose is. Teachers may want to let students make copies of some papers that they would also like to take home.

**THE STUDENTS THEMSELVES** At the end of the school year, portfolio contents can be sent home for parents to see and save, if they wish. Before doing this, teachers may wish to have students prepare a starter portfolio of ideas, writing, plans for reading, and so on, for next year.

***How can I protect against the possible negative effects of allowing a wide variety of persons to see students' portfolios?***

Whatever special reporting the teacher does with portfolios, he or she needs to offset any possible adverse effects by keeping the primary aims for portfolio assessment in mind:

# Questions and Answers *(continued)*

- The overall goal of the program is to develop students as language users. That goal should become the focus of joint student/teacher evaluation of the student's progress.

- Another important goal is for students to develop a habit of self-assessment. That is why the collections must be readily available to students.

- The emphasis should be on examining the process by looking at the product and the way it is produced. Each portfolio should be a working collection containing notes, drafts, and records of the evaluation of its contents.

- The activities assessed should integrate reading, writing, speaking and listening, and viewing and representing.

- The portfolio should be controlled and owned by the student.

- The collections should include reactions to and applications of a variety of text and writing types—with a variety of purposes involving different audiences.

# Further Reading

Arter, Judith A., and Spandel, Vicki. (1992) NCME instructional module: Using portfolios in instruction and assessment. *Educational Measurement: Issues and Practice,* 11 (1), pp. 36–44.
Practical, sequenced steps to a portfolio approach are presented as a training model.

Bishop, Wendy, and Crossley, Gay Lynn. (1993) Not only assessment: Teachers talk about writing portfolios. *Journal of Teaching Writing,* 12 (1), pp. 33–55.
This article shows how using writing-portfolio evaluation changes the way that teachers think about their roles, students, and students' writing. (Whole issue is on portfolios.)

Brown, Sarah. (Spring 1994) Validation of curriculum: Creating a multi-level book as a portfolio and more. *Exercise Exchange,* 39 (2), pp. 29–32.
Project portfolios represent various stages of student growth and writing achievement, result in a published volume of student writing, and validate a curriculum.

Cirincione, Karen M., and Michael, Denise. (October 1994) Changing portfolio process: One journey toward authentic assessment. *Language arts,* 71 (6), pp. 411–418.
Describes how one teacher matched authentic assessment to the instruction in her classroom. (Whole issue is on portfolios.)

Farr, Roger, and Farr, Beverly. (1990) *Language Arts Portfolio Teacher's Manual.* Integrated Assessment System. San Antonio: The Psychological Corporation.
This manual includes descriptions of how to use, rate, and interpret responses to the Integrated Assessment System and several chapters on developing and using portfolios.

Farr, Roger, and Tone, Bruce. (1994) *Portfolio and performance assessment: Helping students evaluate their progress as readers and writers.* Fort Worth: Harcourt Brace College Publishers.
Portfolio assessment and the development of performance assessments is explained in detail with numerous practical suggestions, checklists, and model forms. Working portfolios are recommended to promote students' analysis of their own language use.

Galbraith, Marian, et al. (1994) *Using portfolios to negotiate a rhetorical community.* Report Series 3.10. Albany, New York: National Research Center on Literature Teaching and Learning.
Teacher narration and discussion cover what is required in the negotiation and mentoring involved in becoming a co-assessor with the student of the student's work.

Grady, Emily. (Fall 1992) *The portfolio approach to assessment.* Fastback Series. Bloomington, Indiana: Phi Delta Kappa.
This booklet tells how to use portfolios to assess a wide range of student performance.

Hesse, Douglas. (1993) Portfolios and public discourse: Beyond the academic/personal writing polarity. *Journal of Teaching Writing,* 12 (1), pp. 1–12.
In addition to the writing students do for academic discourse and personal purposes, another kind, public discourse, makes portfolios highly effective. (Whole issue is on portfolios.)

Hewitt, Geof. (1995) *A portfolio primer: Teaching, collecting, and assessing student writing.* Portsmouth, New Hampshire: Heinemann.
This manual on portfolio assessment covers grades 3–12 and a broad range of key considerations, with generous examples from actual portfolios.

Palmer, Barbara C., et al. (1994) *Developing cultural literacy through the writing process: Empowering all learners.* Des Moines: Allyn and Bacon.
Emphasizing cultural literacy, this book addresses each stage of the writing process and treats portfolio assessment. Numerous model activities expand the writer's knowledge base and develop critical thinking.

Porter, Carol, and Cleland, Janell. (1995) *The portfolio as a learning strategy.* Portsmouth, New Hampshire: Heinemann.
Learning strategies involving portfolios and developing self-assessors are described.

Robbins, Sarah, et al. (November 1994) Using portfolio reflections to re-form instructional programs and build curriculum. *English Journal,* 83 (7), pp. 71–78.
English teachers in two schools rely on portfolio assessment to redesign their curricula.

Tierney, Robert J.; Carter, Mark A.; and Desai, Laura E. (1991) *Portfolio assessment in the reading-writing classroom.* Norwood, Massachusetts: Christopher-Gordon.
This presentation covers all aspects of portfolio assessment, relying on research and descriptions of actual implementation.

Valencia, Sheila W., and Place, Nancy. (May 1994) Portfolios: A process for enhancing teaching and learning, *The Reading Teacher,* 47 (8), pp. 666–669.
Aspects of a Bellevue (Washington) project helped teachers use portfolios effectively.

Valencia, Sheila W. (ed.), et al. (1994) *Authentic reading assessment: Practices and possibilities.* Newark, Delaware: International Reading Association.
Case studies describe authentic assessment in and beyond the classroom. Programs at particular schools and in particular states are detailed.

# Summary of My Progress: Writing, Speaking, and Representing

Complete this form before sitting down with your teacher or a classmate to
assess your overall progress, set goals, or discuss specific pieces of your work.

**Grade :** _____     **School year:** _____     **Date of summary:** _____

▶ **What work have I done so far this year?**

Writing:

Speaking:

Representing:

▶ **What project do I plan to work on next?**

Writing:

Speaking:

Representing:

▶ **What do I think of my progress?**

What about my work has improved?

What needs to be better?

▶ **Which examples of work are my favorites and why?**

# Summary of My Progress: Writing, Speaking, and Representing *(continued)*

▶ **Which pieces of work need more revision, and what is needed?**

▶ **How has reading, listening, or viewing helped me in preparing for papers or other projects this year?**

▶ **What a classmate or the teacher thinks about my progress**

In writing—

In speaking—

In representing—

**SELF-EVALUATION**

# Summary of My Progress: Reading, Listening, and Viewing

Complete this form before sitting down with your teacher or a classmate to assess your overall progress; set goals; or discuss specific works you have read, listened to, or watched.

**Grade:** _____ **School year:** _____ **Date of summary:** _____

| ▶ **What have I read, listened to, or watched this year?** | ▶ **What do I plan to read, listen to, or watch next?** |
|---|---|
| Reading: | Reading: |
| Listening: | Listening: |
| Viewing: | Viewing: |
| ▶ **What do I think of my progress in understanding what I read, hear, or see?**<br><br>What about my skills has improved?<br><br><br>What needs to be better? | ▶ **Which things that I've read, listened to, or watched are my favorites and why?** |

# Summary of My Progress: Reading, Listening, and Viewing *(continued)*

▶ **What topics in what I've read, listened to, or watched would I like to explore further? How would I explore these topics?**

▶ **How has writing, speaking, or making media products helped me to become a better reader, listener, or viewer?**

▶ **What a classmate or the teacher thinks about my progress**

In reading—

In listening—

In viewing—

# Self-Evaluation: Any Project

**Grade:** _____   **School year:** _____   **Date of these comments:** _____

▶ **Title of work:** _____   **This is the** _____ **revision.**

The purpose of this work is—

The audience for this work is—

The things I like best about the work are—

The things about the work that do not satisfy me are—

The most difficult thing about writing or creating this work was—

ELEMENTS OF LANGUAGE | First Course | *Assessment Alternatives*

# Peer Evaluation: Any Project

Grade: _____   School year: _____   Date of these comments: _____

▶ **Person whose work I am reviewing:** _____   **Title of work:** _____

This is why the work is (or is not) appropriate for its intended audience:

_____

This work could be improved by adding or explaining these things:

_____

This work could be improved by cutting or replacing these things:

_____

This work could be improved if the following things were reordered:

_____

These are goals that could be considered for the next or a similar project:

These are the comments of _____
[Sign here if your comments are about someone else's paper]

# My Self-Assessment Record

Use this form to evaluate specific pieces of your work, including papers, stories, oral reports, and video projects. Be sure to think carefully about your reasons for assigning ratings to each piece of work.

| **Ratings:** | Needs Improvement | | Acceptable | | Excellent |
|---|---|---|---|---|---|
| | 1 | 2 | 3 | 4 | 5 |

**Title or description of paper or project:**

Rating:

In deciding my rating, what strengths did I see in the paper or project?

What weaknesses did I see in the paper or project?

---

**Title or description of paper or project:**

Rating:

In deciding my rating, what strengths did I see in the paper or project?

What weaknesses did I see in the paper or project?

---

**Title or description of paper or project:**

Rating:

In deciding my rating, what strengths did I see in the paper or project?

What weaknesses did I see in the paper or project?

# Goal-Setting for Reading, Writing, Speaking, Listening, Viewing, or Representing

| ▶ GOAL | ▶ STEPS TO REACH GOAL | ▶ REVIEW OF PROGRESS |
|---|---|---|
| **Reading Goals** | | |
| | | |
| | | |
| | | |
| **Writing Goals** | | |
| | | |
| | | |
| | | |

# Goal-Setting for Reading, Writing, Speaking, Listening, Viewing, or Representing *(continued)*

| ▶ GOAL | ▶ STEPS TO REACH GOAL | ▶ REVIEW OF PROGRESS |
|--------|----------------------|---------------------|
| **Speaking and Listening Goals** | | |
| | | |
| | | |
| | | |
| **Viewing and Representing Goals** | | |
| | | |
| | | |
| | | |

# Student-Teacher Conference Notes

**Name of Teacher** _____

| ▶ Student's notes | ▶ Teacher's notes |
|---|---|
|  |  |

# Table of Contents: How My Portfolio is Organized

Decide on the major categories for work in your portfolio. Then, in the sections below, list the categories you have chosen. The works themselves may be papers, speech notecards, videotapes, multimedia products, or any work you and your teacher agree should be included. In choosing categories, consider organizing work by topic, by genre (essays, poems, stories, and so on), by chronology (work completed by month, for example), by level of difficulty (work that was less difficult, somewhat difficult, and more difficult), or according to another plan.

**Grade:** _____     **School year:** _____

| ▶ WORK IN EACH SECTION | ▶ WHY I PUT THIS WORK IN THIS SECTION |
|---|---|
| **Section 1:** | |
| title: | |
| title: | |
| title: | |
| title: | |
| **Section 2:** | |
| title: | |
| title: | |
| title: | |
| title: | |
| **Section 3:** | |
| title: | |
| title: | |
| title: | |
| title: | |

# About My Portfolio

Use this form whenever you are preparing your portfolio for review by your teacher or another reader.

**Grade:** _____ **School year:** _____ **I began this portfolio on:** _____

▶ **How it is organized:**

_____

▶ **What I think it shows about my progress ...**

_____

as a reader:

_____

as a writer:

_____

as a speaker:

_____

as a listener:

_____

as a viewer of media:

_____

as a maker of media products:

_____

as a critical thinker:

# About My Portfolio *(continued)*

▶ **Examples of My Best Work**

| The best things I have read are— | Why I like them— |
|---|---|
| | |
| The best things I have written are— | Why I like them— |
| | |
| Other things in my portfolio that I hope you notice are—<br><br>1.<br><br><br>2.<br><br><br>3. | What they show— |

**TO PARENT OR GUARDIAN**

# The Portfolio: What Does It Show?

In the left column of the chart below, I have noted what I believe this portfolio shows about your student's development in areas such as reading, writing, speaking, listening, and critical viewing. The right column notes where you can look for evidence of that development.

A prime objective in keeping portfolios is to develop in students a habit of analyzing and evaluating their work. This portfolio includes work that the student has collected over a period of time. The student has decided what to include but has been encouraged to include different types of writing, responses to reading, and evidence of other uses of language. Many of the writings included are accompanied by earlier drafts and plans that show how the work has evolved from a raw idea to a finished piece of writing. The inclusion of drafts is intended to reinforce to the student that using language entails a process of revision and refinement.

| ▶ I believe that this portfolio shows— | ▶ To see evidence of this, please notice— |
| --- | --- |
| | |
| | |
| | |
| | |
| | |

Teacher's signature_____

**TO PARENT OR GUARDIAN**

# Response to the Portfolio

▶ Please answer any questions that seem important to you. Use the reverse side for any additional comments or questions.

Parent or Guardian _____ Date _____

What did you learn from the portfolio about your student's reading?

_____

_____

What did you learn from the portfolio about your student's writing?

_____

_____

Were you surprised by anything in the portfolio? Why?

_____

_____

What do you think is the best thing in the portfolio? What do you like about it?

_____

_____

Do you have questions about anything in the portfolio? What would you like to know more about?

_____

_____

What does the portfolio tell you about your student's progress as a writer, reader, and thinker?

_____

_____

Do you think keeping a portfolio has had an effect on your student as a reader or writer—or in another way? If so, what?

_____

_____

_____

Is there anything missing from the portfolio that you would have liked or had expected to see? If so, what?

_____

_____

# Student Awareness of Language as Process

| Ratings: | 1 = minimal progress | 4 = more progress than expected |
|---|---|---|
| | 2 = less progress than expected | 5 = outstanding progress |
| | 3 = some progress | |

| Processing strategy | Rating | Comments |
|---|---|---|
| Reads, writes, listens, and speaks with a specific purpose; can articulate these purposes | | |
| Tends to appraise what he or she knows about the topic; applies available background knowledge to the task | | |
| Considers clues that indicate what reading or listening may offer; thinks about or preplans expression | | |
| Predicts what is coming next in text or oral presentation; considers what should come next (analyzes writer/ speaker purpose and audience expectation) | | |
| Pictures the meaning being made by reading, writing, listening, and speaking as the process unfolds | | |
| Challenges the ideas, concepts, and details presented to see if they are making sense or are appropriate | | |
| Considers strategy adjustments needed in order to construct clear meaning | | |
| Seeks aid or advice when strategies do not resolve inability to construct clear meaning | | |

# Student Performance Graph

**RATINGS:**   10 = OUTSTANDING PERFORMANCE    8 = GOOD PERFORMANCE    6 = AVERAGE TO ABOVE-AVERAGE PERFORMANCE
     4 = AVERAGE TO BELOW-AVERAGE PERFORMANCE    2 = WEAK PERFORMANCE

| Rating | 1st Grading period | 2nd Grading period | 3rd Grading period | 4th Grading period | 5th Grading period | 6th Grading period | Comments: How much overall progress has this student shown? |
|--------|------|------|------|------|------|------|------|
| 10 | | | | | | | • **Attitude toward using language** |
| 9 | | | | | | | |
| 8 | | | | | | | |
| 7 | | | | | | | ☆ **Involvement in improvement** |
| 6 | | | | | | | |
| 5 | | | | | | | ✕ **Amount/frequency of use** |
| 4 | | | | | | | |
| 3 | | | | | | | |
| 2 | | | | | | | ✓ **Effectiveness of use** |
| 1 | | | | | | | |

**Key Considerations in Growth of Language Use.** Place the appropriate symbol for each category below opposite the rating for each period. Connect the symbols with different colored lines to create a chart.

• **Attitude toward using language**
*How much does the student enjoy reading, writing, speaking, and listening?*

☆ **Involvement in improvement**
*How inclined is the student to self-assess, revise, and set new language-use goals?*

✕ **Amount/frequency of use**
*How often does the student read, write, and speak with a clear purpose?*

✓ **Effectiveness of use**
*How strong is the student's control of language conventions, diction, and style?*
*How effectively does the student use language to complete class work and communicate with others?*

# My Reading Record

> **Ratings:** ✓✓✓✓ Terrific    ✓✓✓ Good    ✓✓ OK    ✓ I didn't like it.

| ▶ Month/ Day | ▶ Title, author fiction or nonfiction | ▶ Notes about what I read | ▶ Rating |
|---|---|---|---|
|  |  |  |  |
|  |  |  |  |
|  |  |  |  |
|  |  |  |  |
|  |  |  |  |
|  |  |  |  |
|  |  |  |  |

**SELF-EVALUATION**

# Inventory: Some Facts About My Reading

| ▶ Questions and answers about my reading | ▶ More about my answers |
|---|---|
| How much do I read? | What kinds of things do I read? |
| How much do I read outside of school/at home? | What kind of reading do I do there? |
| Do I like to read? | Why or why not? |
| Of things I have read, these are my favorites: | Why do I like them best? |
| What topics do I like to read about? | Why do I like reading about these topics? |
| Is anything about reading difficult for me? What? | Why do I think it is difficult? |
| Has reading helped my writing? | Why do I think so? |
| How important is reading? | Why do I think this? |

# Inventory: Some Facts About My Reading Skills

**Title:** _____   **Author:** _____

▶ **Before I Read**

What can I predict will happen in the selection, having looked at illustrations, heads, charts, or maps?

_____

What is my purpose for reading (to interpret, to enjoy, to get information, to solve a problem, etc.)?

_____

What do I already know about the subject of this selection?

_____

How will I adjust my reading rate in order to better understand the selection or book? What kind of resources will I need as I read (dictionary, thesaurus, atlas, etc.)?

_____

▶ **While I Read**

How does what I already know connect with what I'm reading?

_____

What kinds of details do I find interesting? Why?

_____

What questions do I have? Do I need to adjust my predictions? Why?

_____

▶ **After I Read**

What is my reaction to the selection or book? Why?

_____

How were my predictions different from what I found in the selection or book? Why?

_____

# Evaluation of My Reading Skills and Strategies: Narration/Description

**DIRECTIONS** Circle 0, 1, 2, or 3 below to indicate your evaluation of each item.

| | | |
|---|---|---|
| **Evaluation Scale:** | 0 = Not at all | 2 = Some of the time |
| | 1 = I don't know | 3 = Most or all of the time |

## BEFORE READING

**1. Previewing the Text**

- I determine the type of selection or book I am reading (biography, novel, short story, play, folk tale, myth, poem, or personal or descriptive essay).    0   1   2   3

- I look for difficult vocabulary words and decide on an appropriate reading rate.    0   1   2   3

**2. Establishing a Purpose for Reading**

- I identify my purpose for reading (to learn something new, to understand, to interpret, to enjoy, to solve problems).    0   1   2   3

**3. Using Prior Knowledge**

- I consider how my experiences might be connected with the text.    0   1   2   3

- I consider what I know about the author or the genre.    0   1   2   3

- I make predictions about what I will read.    0   1   2   3

## DURING READING

**1. Responding to the Text**

- I think about how my experiences are related to what I'm reading.    0   1   2   3

- I take notes or use graphic organizers.    0   1   2   3

- I identify setting, characters or people, conflicts, and themes.    0   1   2   3

- I use context clues to help me determine meaning.    0   1   2   3

- I identify narrative and descriptive details (the sequence of events, sensory language, and so on).    0   1   2   3

- I make predictions about what will happen next in the text.    0   1   2   3

**2. Monitoring Comprehension**

- I re-read passages when my understanding breaks down.    0   1   2   3

- I read faster or more slowly based on my understanding of the text.    0   1   2   3

# Evaluation of My Reading Skills and Strategies: Narration/Description *(continued)*

**DIRECTIONS** Circle 0, 1, 2, or 3 below to indicate your evaluation of each item.

| **Evaluation Scale:** | 0 = Not at all | 2 = Some of the time |
| --- | --- | --- |
| | 1 = I don't know | 3 = Most or all of the time |

## AFTER READING

### 1. Responding to the Text

- I reflect on the meaning of what I have read and think about how the meaning is connected to my knowledge and experience.    0   1   2   3

- I react to the selection or book and make my own interpretation.    0   1   2   3

- I evaluate my predictions about the reading.    0   1   2   3

- I discuss my thoughts about the selection or book with others.    0   1   2   3

- I extend my reading by choosing another related selection or book to read.    0   1   2   3

- I apply my reading to a paper or project.    0   1   2   3

### 2. Using Study Skills

- I summarize, paraphrase, or outline the selection or book.    0   1   2   3

- I can return to the text and scan for specific information.    0   1   2   3

**Additional Comments:**

# Evaluation of My Reading Skills and Strategies: Exposition

**DIRECTIONS** Circle 0, 1, 2, or 3 below to indicate your evaluation of each item.

| **Evaluation Scale:** | 0 = Not at all | 2 = Some of the time |
|---|---|---|
| | 1 = I don't know | 3 = Most or all of the time |

## BEFORE READING

**1. Previewing the Text**
- I flip through the pages, looking at headings, illustrations, graphs, maps, charts, or other visuals.　　0　1　2　3
- I determine the type of selection or book I am reading (textbook, manual, informative book or article about science, history, geography, etc.).　　0　1　2　3
- I skim the text to examine the difficulty of vocabulary and decide on an appropriate reading rate.　　0　1　2　3

**2. Establishing a Purpose for Reading**
- I set a purpose for reading (to learn something new, to understand, to interpret, to solve problems, to enjoy).　　0　1　2　3
- I write down questions I want answered in the text (*who? what? where? when?* and *how?*).　　0　1　2　3

**3. Using Prior Knowledge**
- I reflect on what I already know about the topic.　　0　1　2　3
- I make predictions about what I will learn from the text and how the text will be organized.　　0　1　2　3

## DURING READING

**1. Responding to the Text**
- I think about what I already know about the topic and how the text supports or contradicts my knowledge.　　0　1　2　3
- I identify main ideas and supporting details.　　0　1　2　3
- I take notes or use graphic organizers to keep track of facts or examples that support the main idea.　　0　1　2　3
- I use graphic organizers to help me sort out a reading's text structure.　　0　1　2　3
- I note all problems and solutions or causes and effects.　　0　1　2　3

# Evaluation of My Reading Skills and Strategies: Exposition *(continued)*

**DIRECTIONS** Circle 0, 1, 2, or 3 below to indicate your evaluation of each item.

| **Evaluation Scale:** | 0 = Not at all | 2 = Some of the time |
|---|---|---|
| | 1 = I don't know | 3 = Most or all of the time |

**Responding to the Text** *(continued)*

- I summarize or paraphrase sections of the selection or book to check my understanding.     0  1  2  3

**2. Monitoring Comprehension**

- I re-read passages when my understanding breaks down.     0  1  2  3

- I read faster or more slowly based on my understanding of the text.     0  1  2  3

**AFTER READING**

**1. Responding to the Text**

- I react to the text and sum up what I've learned.     0  1  2  3

- I evaluate the credibility, or trustworthiness, of the source or text.     0  1  2  3

- I evaluate my predictions about the selection.     0  1  2  3

- I discuss my thoughts about the text with others.     0  1  2  3

- I extend my reading by choosing another related book, article, or other work to read.     0  1  2  3

- I apply my reading to a paper or project.     0  1  2  3

**2. Using Study Skills**

- I summarize, paraphrase, or outline the text's main ideas and supporting details.     0  1  2  3

- I return to the text and scan for specific information.     0  1  2  3

**Additional Comments:**

# Evaluation of My Reading Skills and Strategies: Persuasion

**DIRECTIONS** Circle 0, 1, 2, or 3 below to indicate your evaluation of each item.

| Evaluation Scale: | 0 = Not at all | 2 = Some of the time |
|---|---|---|
| | 1 = I don't know | 3 = Most or all of the time |

## BEFORE READING

**1. Previewing the Text**

- I flip through the pages, looking at headings, illustrations, graphs, maps, charts, or other visuals.  0  1  2  3

- I identify the type of selection I am reading (editorial, review, article, advertisement, etc.).  0  1  2  3

- I skim the text to find difficult vocabulary words and decide on an appropriate reading rate.  0  1  2  3

**2. Establishing a Purpose for Reading**

- I set a purpose for reading (to learn something new, to understand, to interpret, to be persuaded, to solve problems, to enjoy).  0  1  2  3

- I write down questions I want answered in the text (*who? what? where? when?* and *how?*).  0  1  2  3

**3. Using Prior Knowledge**

- I reflect on what I already know about the topic.  0  1  2  3

- I consider what my opinion on the topic might be.  0  1  2  3

- I reflect on what I already know about the author or publication.  0  1  2  3

- I make predictions about what I will learn from the text and what the author's opinion might be.  0  1  2  3

## DURING READING

**1. Responding to the Text**

- I think about what I already know about the topic and how the text supports or contradicts my knowledge.  0  1  2  3

- I identify the author's position statement and supporting reasons and evidence.  0  1  2  3

- I distinguish between facts and opinions.  0  1  2  3

# Evaluation of My Reading Skills and Strategies: Persuasion *(continued)*

▶ **Evaluation Scale:**  
0 = Not at all   2 = Some of the time  
1 = I don't know   3 = Most or all of the time

**Responding to the Text** *(continued)*

- I identify emotional and logical appeals, loaded language, and other persuasive techniques.   0 1 2 3

- I can usually identify logical fallacies such as either-or reasoning, glittering generalities, and so on.   0 1 2 3

- I take notes or use graphic organizers to keep track of facts, examples, or appeals that support the author's position.   0 1 2 3

- I summarize or paraphrase sections of the text to confirm my understanding.   0 1 2 3

**2. Monitoring Comprehension**

- I re-read passages when my understanding breaks down.   0 1 2 3

- I read faster or more slowly based on my understanding of the text.   0 1 2 3

## AFTER READING

**1. Responding to the Text**

- I react to the text and formulate my own opinion.   0 1 2 3

- I summarize the author's purpose and point of view.   0 1 2 3

- I evaluate the credibility, or trustworthiness, of the source or text.   0 1 2 3

- I evaluate my predictions about the text.   0 1 2 3

- I discuss my thoughts about the text with others.   0 1 2 3

- I extend my reading by choosing a related editorial or another work to read.   0 1 2 3

- I apply my reading to a paper or project.   0 1 2 3

**2. Using Study Skills**

- I summarize or outline the author's opinion and supporting details.   0 1 2 3

- I return to the text and scan for specific information and arguments.   0 1 2 3

# Inventory: Some Facts About My Study Skills

| ▶ Questions and answers about my study skills | ▶ More about my answers |
|---|---|
| How often do I study? Do I study at a special time and place? | How do I decide when and where to study? |
| Can I locate the table of contents, the glossary, and the index of my textbook? | How might these parts of the textbook help me study? |
| Do I preview or skim major sections of the text I'm reading? | How can previewing or skimming help me? |
| Do I review the maps, tables, and other graphic organizers in the texts that I study? | What help do these features provide? |
| Do I notice features such as bullets, headings, and subheadings? | How do these features help my understanding? |
| Do I use a dictionary, encyclopedia, or other reference materials in my studying? | Why or why not? |
| Do I ask myself questions about the text as I read? Do I use the study questions in my textbooks? | Why is asking questions important? |

# Inventory: Some Facts About My Study Skills *(continued)*

| ▶ Questions and answers about my study skills | ▶ More about my answers |
|---|---|
| Do I use study strategies such as SQ3R or creating graphic organizers? | How do these strategies help me? |
| Do I practice making generalizations or drawing conclusions? | How does this help my understanding? |
| Do I distinguish between fact and opinion? | Why is it important to notice this difference? |
| Do I note causes and effects or problems and solutions in the texts I read? | Why is understanding these relationships helpful to my studying? |
| Do I make the necessary adjustments in my studying based on my reading rate? | Why is my reading rate important in studying? |
| Are my study habits successful? | Why or why not? |

# Progress in Reading

**Ratings:**

| 1 = minimal progress | 4 = more progress than expected |
|---|---|
| 2 = less progress than expected | 5 = outstanding progress |
| 3 = some progress | |

| Volume of reading | Rating | Comments |
|---|---|---|
| Compared with last progress report | | |
| Amount student is reading during unscheduled school time | | |
| Amount student is reading outside of school | | |
| Has read from a variety of genres and sources such as diaries, newspapers, electronic texts, and speeches | | |

| Interests growing out of and promoting reading | Rating | Comments |
|---|---|---|
| Interest in some topics has intensified | | |
| Has read texts on a variety of topics | | |
| Is developing clear preferences in reading | | |
| Shares ideas and stories from texts read | | |
| Appears to be more questioning; turns to texts for answers | | |

# Progress in Reading *(continued)*

| Attitudes about reading | Rating | Comments |
|---|---|---|
| Reads assignments without resistance | | |
| Talks about favorite books, stories, articles; cites texts read; reacts openly to what has been read in class | | |
| Is actively involved in portfolio self-assessment of reading | | |
| Has improved perception of self as a reader; demonstrates confidence with texts and ideas | | |

| Applied comprehension | Rating | Comments |
|---|---|---|
| Relates reading to experience and background | | |
| Reading appears to be promoting improvement in writing and speaking | | |
| Expresses and shows appreciation for new ideas | | |

| Reading strategies | Rating | Comments |
|---|---|---|
| Thinks of reading as a process | | |
| Appears to read more fluently | | |
| Has strategies to seek help if needed | | |
| Has a growing lexicon/vocabulary | | |

**TEACHER'S REPORT**

# Progress in Reading Skills

| **Ratings:** | 1 = minimal progress | 4 = more progress than expected |
|---|---|---|
| | 2 = less progress than expected | 5 = outstanding progress |
| | 3 = some progress | |

| Comprehension skills | Rating | Comments |
|---|---|---|
| Can identify main ideas and details | | |
| After reading, can recall many details accurately | | |
| Uses context clues to define difficult vocabulary | | |
| Recognizes and understands common abbreviations, symbols, and acronyms | | |
| Can identify correctly the antecedents of pronouns | | |
| Can follow written instructions | | |
| Can follow sequences of events | | |
| Can identify and follow common text structures such as compare/contrast and cause/effect | | |
| Recognizes common genres and can identify some distinguishing features of each | | |

# Progress in Reading Skills *(continued)*

| Interpretive skills | Rating | Comments |
|---|---|---|
| Can make logical predictions | | |
| Can connect own knowledge and experience to the text | | |
| Uses context clues to decipher meaning | | |
| Can interpret character traits and relationships in fiction | | |
| Can understand implied cause-and-effect relationships, implied main ideas, and implied sequences of events | | |
| Can make generalizations and draw conclusions about a text | | |
| Can decipher the meaning of abstract words and/or multiple-meaning words | | |
| Can interpret figurative language | | |
| Can accurately summarize a text | | |
| Reads with an understanding of literary concepts such as plot and theme | | |
| In nonfiction, can identify an author's purpose and point of view | | |
| Can synthesize information from more than one source | | |

# Progress in Reading Skills *(continued)*

| Critical thinking skills | Rating | Comments |
|---|---|---|
| Can differentiate fact from opinion | | |
| Can assess the credibility of an author | | |
| Can recognize logical and emotional appeals and identify their purpose in a text | | |
| Can recognize bias | | |
| Can interpret persuasive and propaganda techniques and identify their purpose in a text | | |
| Can detect fallacies in reasoning | | |
| Can distinguish between relevant and irrelevant material in a text | | |

# Record of My Writing

| Ratings: | ✓✓✓✓ One of my best! | ✓✓ OK, but not my best |
|---|---|---|
| | ✓✓✓ Better if I revise it | ✓ I don't like this one. |

| ▶ Month/Day | ▶ Title and type of writing | ▶ Notes about this piece of writing | ▶ Rating |
|---|---|---|---|
| | | | |
| | | | |
| | | | |
| | | | |
| | | | |
| | | | |
| | | | |

# My Spelling Log

| ▶ Word | ▶ My misspelling | ▶ How to remember correct spelling |
| --- | --- | --- |
|  |  |  |
|  |  |  |
|  |  |  |
|  |  |  |
|  |  |  |
|  |  |  |
|  |  |  |
|  |  |  |
|  |  |  |
|  |  |  |
|  |  |  |
|  |  |  |
|  |  |  |
|  |  |  |
|  |  |  |
|  |  |  |
|  |  |  |
|  |  |  |
|  |  |  |

**SELF-EVALUATION**

# My Vocabulary Log

Put a circle around any of the words on your list that you often use in writing or speaking. Underline any of the words on your list that you frequently come across in reading.

> **Ratings:** ☆ = a word that you want to remember and use in writing or speaking
> + = a word you want to recognize when you come across it in reading

| Word | Brief definition or synonym | Sentence the word was used in | Rating |
|---|---|---|---|
| | | | |
| | | | |
| | | | |
| | | | |
| | | | |
| | | | |
| | | | |
| | | | |
| | | | |
| | | | |
| | | | |
| | | | |
| | | | |
| | | | |
| | | | |

# Inventory: Some Facts About My Writing

| ▶ Questions and answers about my writing | ▶ More about my answers |
|---|---|
| How often do I write? | What types of writing do I do? |
| Do I write outside of school/at home? | What kind of writing do I do there? |
| Do I like to write? | Why or why not? |
| Of the things I have written, I like these best: | Why do I like them best? |
| What topics do I like to write about? | Why do I like to write about these topics? |
| Is anything about writing difficult for me? What? | Why do I think it is difficult? |
| Does reading help me to be a better writer, or vice versa? | Why do I think this? |
| How important is learning to write well? | Why do I think this? |

# Evaluating Your Writing Process

Choose one paper from your portfolio. Track your writing process for that paper by writing brief answers to these questions. Keep the questions and your answers in your portfolio.

## ▶ PREWRITING

**1.** How did you decide on your subject?

**2.** Did you use any of the prewriting techniques you have learned in class? Which ones? How did they work for you with this assignment?

**3.** Did you plan the organization of your paper before you started writing? Why or why not?

**4.** What did you like best about this stage of the assignment? What did you like least?

**5.** About how much time did you spend on this stage of the writing process?

## ▶ WRITING

**6.** What did you find easiest about writing your draft?

**7.** What did you find most difficult about writing your draft?

**8.** What was your main concern while writing the draft? Organization? Style? Development of ideas? Something else? Why?

**9.** What did you like best about this stage of the writing process?

**10.** About how much time did you spend writing your draft?

# Evaluating Your Writing Process *(continued)*

▶ **EVALUATING AND REVISING**

**11.** Did you receive feedback on your draft from anyone? If so, was the feedback helpful? Why or why not?

**12.** What did you think about your first draft? Why?

**13.** In this stage, did you make any major changes to your draft? Why or why not?

**14.** What did you like best about this stage of the writing process? What did you like least?

**15.** About how much time did you spend evaluating and revising your draft?

▶ **PROOFREADING, PUBLISHING, AND REFLECTING**

**16.** How did you proofread your paper and design its appearance? How long did this take?

**17.** Where did you publish your paper? If you published your paper by reading it aloud, who was your audience?

**18.** What did you like best about this stage of the writing process? What did you like least?

**19.** On which stage of the writing process did you spend the most time? How did spending this time affect the quality of your final paper?

**20.** What will you do differently the next time you write? What will you do the same way?

# Assessing Your Writing Process: Analytic Scale

Choose one paper from your portfolio, preferably one for which you have your prewriting notes and all your drafts. Use the chart below to analyze your writing process. Circle the numbers that most clearly indicate how well your writing process meets the stated criteria. The lowest possible total score is 5, the highest, 20.

**1** = Does not achieve these criteria

**2** = Made some effort to meet these criteria but with little success

**3** = Made a serious effort to meet these criteria and was fairly successful

**4** = Clearly meets these criteria

**Title of paper** _____

| ▶ STAGE IN WRITING PROCESS | ▶ CRITERIA FOR EVALUATION | ▶ RATING |
|---|---|---|
| **Prewriting** | ■ Used prewriting techniques to find and limit subject and to gather details about subject<br>■ Organized details in a reasonable way | 1  2  3  4 |
| **Writing** | ■ Got most of ideas down on paper in a rough draft | 1  2  3  4 |
| **Revising** | ■ Did complete peer or self-evaluation<br>■ Found ways to improve content, organization, and style of rough draft<br>■ Revised by adding, cutting, replacing, and moving material | 1  2  3  4 |
| **Proofreading** | ■ Corrected errors in spelling, grammar, usage, punctuation, capitalization, and manuscript form | 1  2  3  4 |
| **Publishing and Reflecting** | ■ Produced a clean final copy in proper form<br>■ Shared the piece of writing with others<br>■ Reflected on the writing process and on the paper's strengths and weaknesses | 1  2  3  4 |

**Additional Comments:**

# Evaluating and Revising Your Draft

Read through your draft using the following five steps as a guide. Answer each question fully and thoughtfully.

**Title of paper** _____

---

▶ **STEP 1: THINKING ABOUT YOUR READERS**

How do you want your readers to react to your paper?

Read through your paper quickly without stopping. Then, state what you think the readers' reactions will be.

If the readers' reactions are likely to be different than the reaction you want, what do you need to change in the paper?

---

▶ **STEP 2: LOOKING AT YOUR INTRODUCTION**

Look closely at the introduction to your paper. What does the introduction do to capture the readers' interest?

What do you like best about your introduction?

What do you like least?

What might you add, cut, replace, or reorder to strengthen your introduction?

# Evaluating and Revising Your Draft *(continued)*

▶ **STEP 3: LOOKING AT THE BODY**

Read carefully through the body of your paper. What main points or ideas do you want your readers to understand?

Do you think the reader will consider the order of your ideas or points logical? Explain.

What examples of vivid, precise, or persuasive language do you find in the body of the essay?

Does this assignment call for examples and facts? If so, what examples and facts have you used?

Where might additional facts and examples be helpful?

Do any facts or examples seem unrelated or unnecessary? Why?

What might you add, cut, replace, or reorder to strengthen the body of the paper?

# Evaluating and Revising Your Draft (continued)

## STEP 4: LOOKING AT THE CONCLUSION

Look closely at the conclusion of your paper. What does the conclusion do to bring the paper to a satisfactory close?

What do you like best about your conclusion?

What do you like least?

What might you add, cut, replace, or reorder to strengthen your conclusion?

## STEP 5: HEARING HOW THE PAPER SOUNDS

Read your paper aloud. Which sentences sound especially good to you?

Which sentences seem awkward, wordy, or unclear?

What words or phrases might you add, cut, replace, or reorder to strengthen those sentences?

# Checklist: Evaluating and Revising Your Draft

Revise your paper until you can answer *yes* to each of the following questions.
Add, cut, replace, or reorder material in your paper as necessary.

**Title of paper** _____

| Content | Yes | No |
|---|---|---|
| Does the introduction grab the reader's interest? | | |
| Is the introduction clear and logical? | | |
| From the beginning of the paper to the end, are the subject and purpose of the paper clear? | | |
| Is the body of the paper well developed? | | |
| Is each main point in the paper elaborated with facts, details, or other support? | | |
| Is the paper free of unrelated or unnecessary ideas? | | |
| Is the paper interesting? | | |
| Does the paper end in a way that is satisfying to the reader? | | |
| Does the paper achieve its purpose? (Before you answer, take a moment to recall the paper's purpose as clearly as possible.) | | |

| Organization | Yes | No |
|---|---|---|
| Are the ideas and details arranged in a clear and logical order? | | |
| Have transitions been used to make clear the relationships between sentences and paragraphs? | | |

| Style | Yes | No |
|---|---|---|
| Is every sentence in the paper clear and smoothly written? | | |
| Is the language of the paper appropriate for its audience and purpose? | | |
| Have you avoided choppy and wordy sentences? Have you varied your sentence lengths and structures? | | |

**Additional Notes:**

# Evaluating Your Content and Organization

**Writer's name** _____ **Title of paper** _____

---

▶ **Introduction**

The best thing about the introduction is—

To improve the introduction, the writer might—

---

▶ **Body**

The two best things about the body are—

The body's organization is or is not clear because—

To improve the body, the writer might—

---

▶ **Conclusion**

The best thing about the conclusion is—

To improve the conclusion, the writer might—

---

▶ **Overall Evaluation**

What does this writer do best of all?

Check the element that the writer should concentrate most on when revising.

_____ Interest Level       _____ Style       _____ Organization       _____ Development of Ideas

# Evaluating Your Audience and Purpose

**Writer's name** _____   **Title of paper** _____

---

**STEP 1: Evaluating for Audience**

Who is the intended audience of the paper?

What information, ideas, or attitudes are they likely to have about the subject of the paper?

Has the writer taken the audience's knowledge, ideas, and attitudes into account? How can you tell?

Considering the audience, does the writer need to add material to the paper or delete material from the paper? If so, what?

---

**STEP 2: Evaluating for Purpose**

What is the purpose of the paper?

What are some characteristics that papers with that purpose usually have?

Which of those characteristics does this paper have? Give examples.

Which of those characteristics (if any) are missing from this paper? What reasons might the writer have for not including those characteristics?

How successful is the writer in achieving the purpose? What might help the writer more fully meet the purpose?

---

**STEP 3: Overall Evaluation**

What is the most important thing the writer needs to do to be certain of achieving his or her purpose with this audience?

# Revising: Your Response as a Reader

**Writer's name** _____  **Title of paper** _____

1. Which part of the paper did you find most interesting? Why? _____

   _____

   _____

2. Which part of the paper might the writer make more interesting? _____

   _____

   How would you suggest that the writer do this? _____

   _____

3. What is the writer's purpose? How can you tell? _____

   _____

   Do you think the writer is successful in achieving the purpose? Explain. _____

   _____

   _____

4. Are any parts of the paper difficult to read or understand? If so, which ones and why?

   _____

   _____

5. Does the paper need further editing and proofreading? Explain.

   _____

   _____

6. When the writer revises, is there anything that he or she definitely should not change?

   _____

   _____

7. Suggest two specific things the writer could do to improve the paper.

   _____

   _____

8. Tell the writer what he or she did well or what you will remember about this paper.

   _____

   _____

# Four-Point Analytic Scale for Revising

Read the following list of criteria for good writing. Then, with these criteria in mind, read your classmate's paper. Finally, for each criterion, rate the writing assignment from 1 to 4. The lowest possible total score is 12, the highest, 48.

**1** = Does not achieve this standard

**2** = Shows some effort to meet this standard but with little success

**3** = Shows a serious effort to meet this standard and was fairly successful

**4** = Clearly meets this standard

Be ready to discuss your evaluation with the writer and to make suggestions for revision.

**Writer's name** _____  **Title of paper** _____

| Criteria for Evaluation | Rating | | | |
|---|---|---|---|---|
| ▪ The writing is interesting. | 1 | 2 | 3 | 4 |
| ▪ The writing achieves its purpose. | 1 | 2 | 3 | 4 |
| ▪ The writing contains enough details. | 1 | 2 | 3 | 4 |
| ▪ The writing does not contain unrelated ideas. | 1 | 2 | 3 | 4 |
| ▪ The ideas and details are arranged in an effective order. | 1 | 2 | 3 | 4 |
| ▪ The connections between ideas and between sentences are clear. | 1 | 2 | 3 | 4 |
| ▪ The writer's meaning is clear throughout. | 1 | 2 | 3 | 4 |
| ▪ The language fits the audience and purpose of the piece of writing. | 1 | 2 | 3 | 4 |
| ▪ The sentences read smoothly. | 1 | 2 | 3 | 4 |
| ▪ The paper is free (or almost free) of problems in grammar and usage. | 1 | 2 | 3 | 4 |
| ▪ The paper is free (or almost free) of problems in punctuation, capitalization, and spelling. | 1 | 2 | 3 | 4 |
| ▪ The paper is free (or almost free) of problems in manuscript form. | 1 | 2 | 3 | 4 |
| **Total:** | | | | |

# General Analytic Scale

The points possible for each of the twelve criteria listed in the chart may vary depending on the writing assignment that is being evaluated. Your teacher may give you the points possible for each category. Or, for some assignments, your teacher may give you the responsibility of deciding the points possible.

After you have filled out the **Points Possible** column, read the paper (your own or a classmate's) carefully and thoughtfully. Complete the **Points Given** column and tally the score.

**Writer's name**_____ **Title of paper**_____

| CRITERIA FOR EVALUATION | Points Possible | Points Given |
|---|---|---|
| **Content** | | |
| Is the writing interesting? | | |
| Does the writing achieve its purpose? | | |
| Are there enough details? | | |
| Are the ideas related to the topic? | | |
| **Organization** | | |
| Are ideas and details arranged in an effective order? | | |
| Are the connections between ideas, sentences, and paragraphs clear? | | |
| **Style** | | |
| Is the meaning of each sentence clear? | | |
| Are the language and tone appropriate for the audience, topic, and purpose? | | |
| Do sentences read smoothly? | | |
| **Grammar and Usage** | | |
| Is the paper relatively free of problems in grammar and usage? | | |
| **Punctuation, Capitalization, and Spelling** | | |
| Is the paper relatively free of problems in punctuation, capitalization, and spelling? | | |
| **Manuscript Form** | | |
| Is the paper relatively free of problems in manuscript form? | | |
| **Total Points:** | | |

# Four-Point Analytic Scale: General

Circle the numbers that most clearly indicate how well the paper meets the stated criteria. Total the numbers circled. The lowest possible score is 15, the highest, 60.

**1** = The paper clearly does not achieve this standard.

**2** = The paper indicates that the writer has made some effort to meet this standard but with little success.

**3** = The paper indicates that the writer has made a serious effort to meet this standard and that he or she has been fairly successful.

**4** = The paper clearly meets this standard.

**Writer's name** _____  **Title of paper**_____

### Content

| | | | | |
|---|---|---|---|---|
| ■ The writing is likely to interest the intended audience. | 1 | 2 | 3 | 4 |
| ■ The writing has a clear purpose and achieves that purpose. | 1 | 2 | 3 | 4 |
| ■ The writing is unified and clear. | 1 | 2 | 3 | 4 |
| ■ The subject has been as completely explored and elaborated as possible. | 1 | 2 | 3 | 4 |
| ■ The writing does not contain unrelated or distracting details. | 1 | 2 | 3 | 4 |

### Organization

| | | | | |
|---|---|---|---|---|
| ■ The writing has a clear structure. | 1 | 2 | 3 | 4 |
| ■ Ideas and details are arranged in an effective and logical order. | 1 | 2 | 3 | 4 |
| ■ The connections between and among ideas are clear. | 1 | 2 | 3 | 4 |

### Style

| | | | | |
|---|---|---|---|---|
| ■ The language suits the topic, audience, purpose, and occasion. | 1 | 2 | 3 | 4 |
| ■ The sentences are graceful and not awkward. | 1 | 2 | 3 | 4 |
| ■ The paper avoids wordiness, clichés, jargon, and other style problems. | 1 | 2 | 3 | 4 |
| ■ The writer's meaning is clear throughout. | 1 | 2 | 3 | 4 |

### Grammar, Usage, and Mechanics

| | | | | |
|---|---|---|---|---|
| ■ The paper is relatively free of problems in grammar and usage. | 1 | 2 | 3 | 4 |
| ■ The paper is relatively free of errors in spelling and mechanics. | 1 | 2 | 3 | 4 |
| ■ The paper follows correct manuscript form. | 1 | 2 | 3 | 4 |

**Total:** _____

# Open Analytic Scale

**Writer's name** _____ **Title of paper** _____

| EVALUATION CRITERIA | Points Possible | Points Given |
|---|---|---|
| **Content:** | 20<br><br>*or*<br><br>_____ | |
| **Organization:** | 20<br><br>*or*<br><br>_____ | |
| **Style:** | 20<br><br>*or*<br><br>_____ | |
| **Grammar and Usage:** | 20<br><br>*or*<br><br>_____ | |
| **Spelling, Punctuation, and Manuscript Form:** | 20<br><br>*or*<br><br>_____ | |
| **Total Points:** | 100 | |

# Analytic Scale: An Eyewitness Account

Circle the numbers that clearly indicate how well the eyewitness account meets the stated criteria. Total the numbers circled. The lowest possible score is 15, the highest, 60.

**1** = The essay clearly does not achieve this standard.

**2** = The essay indicates that the writer has made some effort to meet this standard but with little success.

**3** = The paper indicates that the writer has made a serious effort to meet this standard and that he or she has been fairly successful.

**4** = The paper clearly meets this standard.

**Writer's name** _____　**Title of paper** _____

**▶ Organization**

| | | | | |
|---|---|---|---|---|
| The events of the experience are arranged in chronological order. | 1 | 2 | 3 | 4 |
| Connections between the details are clear. | 1 | 2 | 3 | 4 |
| The account's organization is clear and easy to follow. | 1 | 2 | 3 | 4 |

**▶ Content**

| | | | | |
|---|---|---|---|---|
| The introduction includes a salutation and a question, story, or personal note that will grab the reader's attention. | 1 | 2 | 3 | 4 |
| The account provides any needed background information. | 1 | 2 | 3 | 4 |
| The writer shares his or her thoughts, feelings, and questions about the experience. | 1 | 2 | 3 | 4 |
| The writer includes relevant details, vivid descriptions, dialogue, or figures of speech. | 1 | 2 | 3 | 4 |
| The conclusion summarizes the importance of the experience. | 1 | 2 | 3 | 4 |
| The account closes with a personal note to the reader. | 1 | 2 | 3 | 4 |

**▶ Style**

| | | | | |
|---|---|---|---|---|
| The account uses precise nouns and adjectives. | 1 | 2 | 3 | 4 |
| The writer's tone and voice are appropriate for the purpose and audience. | 1 | 2 | 3 | 4 |
| Sentences are varied in structure and length throughout the account. | 1 | 2 | 3 | 4 |

**▶ Grammar, Usage, and Mechanics**

| | | | | |
|---|---|---|---|---|
| The account is relatively free of problems in grammar and usage. | 1 | 2 | 3 | 4 |
| The account is relatively free of errors in spelling and mechanics. | 1 | 2 | 3 | 4 |
| The writer correctly punctuates dialogue. | 1 | 2 | 3 | 4 |

**Total Points:** _____

# Analytic Scale: Instructions

Read the instructions (your own or a classmate's) carefully and thoughtfully. Then, read each of the following criteria and complete the **Points Given** column. When you are finished, tally the score.

**Writer's name** _____ **Title of paper** _____

| CRITERIA FOR EVALUATION | Points Possible | Points Given |
|---|---|---|
| **Organization** | | |
| Are the steps arranged in chronological order? | 5 | |
| Are the steps connected with clear transitional words and phrases? | 5 | |
| Is the organization logical and easy to follow? | 10 | |
| **Content** | | |
| Does the introduction engage the reader and provide a clear statement of the topic? | 10 | |
| Does the writer give a reason for learning the activity or process? | 10 | |
| Does the writer provide a list of necessary materials? | 10 | |
| Are all details relevant to the process and fully elaborated? | 10 | |
| Does the conclusion restate the reason for learning the process and end with some parting advice? | 10 | |
| **Style** | | |
| Do the instructions contain prepositional phrases that help the reader see transitions between ideas? | 5 | |
| Is the writer's tone appropriate for the audience, purpose, and occasion? | 5 | |
| Are the instructions clearly and concisely written? | 5 | |
| **Grammar, Usage, and Mechanics** | | |
| Are the instructions relatively free of problems in grammar and usage? | 5 | |
| Are the instructions relatively free of errors in spelling and mechanics? | 5 | |
| Does the writer correctly use commas with introductory prepositional phrases? | 5 | |
| **Total Points:** | 100 | |

# Analytic Scale: An Advantages/Disadvantages Essay

Use the chart below to evaluate an advantages/disadvantages essay. Circle the numbers that most clearly indicate how well the essay meets the stated criteria. The lowest possible total score is 10, the highest, 40.

**1** = Does not achieve this standard

**2** = Made some effort to meet this standard but with little success

**3** = Made a serious effort to meet this standard and was fairly successful

**4** = Clearly meets this standard

Writer's name _____　Title of paper_____

| ▶ WRITING ELEMENT | ▶ CRITERIA FOR EVALUATION | ▶ RATING |
|---|---|---|
| ▶ **Organization** | ■ Details are arranged by listing all advantages together and all disadvantages together. | 1　2　3　4 |
| | ■ The essay's organization is easy to follow and understand. | 1　2　3　4 |
| ▶ **Content** | ■ The introduction grabs the reader's attention and includes a main idea statement. | 1　2　3　4 |
| | ■ The body paragraphs clearly discuss both advantages and disadvantages. | 1　2　3　4 |
| | ■ The essay includes explanations and elaborated support for each advantage and disadvantage. | 1　2　3　4 |
| | ■ The conclusion summarizes the information and restates the thesis, but does not include an opinion. | 1　2　3　4 |
| ▶ **Style** | ■ The essay does not contain stringy sentences. | 1　2　3　4 |
| | ■ The writer's tone is appropriate for the essay's audience and informative purpose. | 1　2　3　4 |
| ▶ **Grammar, Usage, and Mechanics** | ■ The essay is relatively free of grammar and usage, spelling, and mechanics errors. | 1　2　3　4 |
| | ■ The writer uses correct punctuation to avoid run-on sentences when combining sentences. | 1　2　3　4 |
| | **Total Points:** | |

# Analytic Scale: A Jacket for a Novel

Evaluate a book jacket by awarding points for how well the project meets the following criteria. Total the numbers in the **Points Given** column to determine an overall score.

**Writer's name** _____ **Title of paper** _____

| CRITERIA FOR EVALUATION | Points Possible | Points Given |
|---|---|---|
| **Organization** | | |
| ■ Book covers and flaps are arranged according to the writing framework in the pupil's edition. | 20 *or* | |
| ■ The organization is clear and easy to follow. | ____ | |
| **Content** | | |
| ■ The back flap contains author information. | 50 *or* | |
| ■ The back cover has a catchy quotation or passage. | ____ | |
| ■ The front cover includes the book's title and author. | | |
| ■ The front cover has a meaningful, attention-grabbing image. | | |
| ■ The front flap has a statement that hooks the reader. | | |
| ■ The front flap contains a story summary, including details on characters, setting, plot, and theme. | | |
| ■ The front flap gives a reason for reading the novel. | | |
| **Style** | | |
| ■ The book cover contains a variety of sentence lengths. | 15 *or* | |
| ■ The book cover's text and layout achieve their informative and persuasive purposes. | ____ | |
| **Grammar, Usage, and Mechanics** | | |
| ■ The book cover is relatively free of grammar, usage, spelling and mechanics errors. | 15 *or* | |
| ■ The text of the book cover includes correct hyphenation. | ____ | |
| **Total Points:** | 100 | |

**PEER AND SELF-EVALUATION**

# Analytic Scale: A Report of Information

Rate how well the informative report meets the following criteria on a scale of
1 to 5, with 1 being the lowest rating and 5 being the highest. When you are
finished, add the numbers. The lowest possible score is 12, the highest, 60.

**Writer's name** _____  **Title of paper**_____

**Criteria for Evaluation:** _____  **Rating (1 to 5):**

1. The introduction grabs the audience's attention.                                    _____

2. The introduction provides a main idea (thesis) statement that covers
   all the report's important ideas.                                                   _____

3. Each paragraph addresses a different main point.                                     _____

4. The report answers all relevant *5W-How?* questions.                                 _____

5. The writer includes relevant details (facts, statistics, and examples) to
   support each paragraph's main point.                                                _____

6. The conclusion restates the report's main idea, and refers back to the
   introduction or draws a thoughtful conclusion.                                       _____

7. The writer organizes his or her ideas in a logical order.                            _____

8. The writer lists at least three different types of sources used in researching
   the report.                                                                          _____

9. The report's sources are reliable.                                                   _____

10. The writer varies sentence beginnings.                                              _____

11. The report is relatively free of grammar, usage, and mechanics errors.              _____

12. The writer has correctly formatted all sources in the Works Cited list.             _____

**Total Points:**  _____

# Analytic Scale: A Persuasive Essay

Circle the numbers on the scales that indicate how well the persuasive paper meets the stated criteria. Then, total the numbers circled. The lowest possible score is 15, the highest, 45.

> **Ratings:**   1 = Does not meet this standard
> 2 = Made some effort at meeting this standard
> 3 = Clearly meets this standard

**Writer's name** _____   **Title of paper** _____

## Organization

- Reasons are arranged in a logical and persuasive order.          1   2   3
- The essay's organization is clear and easy to follow.            1   2   3

## Content

- The introduction grabs the reader's attention.                  1   2   3
- The writer includes a clear opinion statement.                  1   2   3
- The writer gives at least two reasons to support his or her opinion.   1   2   3
- Each reason is supported by at least one piece of convincing evidence.  1   2   3
- The writer effectively addresses counterarguments.             1   2   3
- The conclusion restates the writer's opinion.                  1   2   3
- The conclusion summarizes the reasons or gives a call to action.   1   2   3

## Style

- The essay is free of clichés.                                   1   2   3
- The writer's tone is appropriate for the audience and purpose.  1   2   3
- The essay's sentences are varied in structure and length.       1   2   3

## Grammar, Usage, and Mechanics

- The essay is relatively free of problems in grammar and usage.  1   2   3
- The essay is relatively free of problems in spelling and mechanics.  1   2   3
- The writer correctly uses comparative modifiers.                1   2   3

**Total Points:** _____

# Analytic Scale: A Print Advertisement

Use the following questions to evaluate a print advertisement. Read the advertisement carefully. Then, award points for each criterion based on the number of points possible. Finally, add the points in the **Points Given** column to determine a final score.

**Writer's name** _____          **Title of paper** _____

| CRITERIA FOR EVALUATION | Points Possible | Points Given |
|---|---|---|
| ■ Does the image use color and people or objects to catch the reader's attention? | 10 | |
| ■ Is the slogan catchy and memorable? | 5 | |
| ■ Does the ad have a clearly defined target audience? | 10 | |
| ■ Does the ad name the product or service and provide a clear description? | 10 | |
| ■ Does the ad use one or more effective persuasive techniques? | 10 | |
| ■ Does the ad give logical reasons for buying the product or service? | 10 | |
| ■ Does the ad provide important facts about the product or service? | 10 | |
| ■ Does the ad clearly tell readers what action to take to buy the product or service? | 5 | |
| ■ Is the organization of the ad easy to follow? | 5 | |
| ■ Is the writer's tone appropriate for the audience and purpose? | 5 | |
| ■ Does the writer use emotional language? | 5 | |
| ■ Is the paper relatively free of grammar and usage problems? | 5 | |
| ■ Is the paper relatively free of spelling and mechanics errors? | 5 | |
| ■ Does the writer correctly punctuate possessives? | 5 | |
| **Total Points:** | 100 | |

# Proofreading Review

Proofread your paper using each of the following steps. Put a check by each step after you complete it.

_____ **1.** Read the paper backward word by word.

_____ **2.** Make a large card with a one- or two-inch-sized strip cut into it and read every word in the paper, one at a time, through the hole.

_____ **3.** Read the first sentence in your paper carefully. Put your left index finger on the punctuation mark that signals the end of that sentence. Now, put your right index finger on the punctuation mark that ends the second sentence. Carefully read the material between your fingers; then, move your left index finger to the end of the second sentence, your right to the end of the third sentence and read carefully. Keep moving your fingers until you have carefully examined each sentence in the paper.

List the mistakes you discovered when proofreading.

_____

_____

_____

_____

_____

_____

_____

_____

_____

_____

_____

_____

_____

_____

_____

# Proofreading Checklist

Read through the paper and then mark the following statements either **T** for true or **F** for false. Return the paper and checklist to the writer. Give the writer time to locate and correct the errors. After the writer has done his or her best to correct the paper, offer to assist if your help is needed.

**Writer's name** _____ **Title of paper** _____

_____ 1. The paper is neat.

_____ 2. Each sentence begins with a capital letter.

_____ 3. Each sentence ends with a period, question mark, or exclamation mark.

_____ 4. Each sentence is complete. Each has a subject and a predicate and expresses a complete thought.

_____ 5. Run-on sentences are avoided.

_____ 6. A singular verb is used with each singular subject and a plural verb with each plural subject.

_____ 7. Nominative case pronouns such as *I* and *we* are used for subjects; objective case pronouns such as *me* and *us* are used for objects.

_____ 8. Singular pronouns are used to refer to singular nouns, and plural pronouns are used to refer to plural nouns.

_____ 9. Indefinite pronoun references are avoided.

_____ 10. Each word is spelled correctly.

_____ 11. Frequently confused verbs such as *lie/lay, sit/set, rise/raise, all ready/already,* and *fewer/less* are used correctly.

_____ 12. Double negatives are avoided.

_____ 13. All proper nouns and proper adjectives are capitalized.

_____ 14. Word endings such as *–s, –ing,* and *–ed* are included where they should be.

_____ 15. No words have been accidentally left out or accidentally written twice.

_____ 16. Each paragraph is indented.

_____ 17. Apostrophes are used correctly with contractions and possessive nouns.

_____ 18. Commas or pairs of commas are used correctly.

_____ 19. Dialogue is punctuated and capitalized correctly.

_____ 20. Any correction that could not be rewritten or retyped is crossed out with a single line.

# My Record of Proofreading Corrections

Keeping a record of your mistakes can be helpful. For the next few writing assignments, list the errors you, your teacher, or your peers find in your work. If you faithfully use this kind of record, you'll find it easier to avoid troublesome errors.

**Writer's name** _____  **Title of paper** _____

**Write sentences that contain errors in grammar or usage here.**     **Write corrections here.**

_____     _____

_____     _____

_____     _____

_____     _____

_____     _____

_____     _____

_____     _____

_____     _____

**Write sentences that contain errors in mechanics here.**     **Write corrections here.**

_____     _____

_____     _____

_____     _____

_____     _____

_____     _____

_____     _____

_____     _____

**Write misspelled words and corrections here.**

_____  _____  _____  _____

_____  _____  _____  _____

_____  _____  _____  _____

_____  _____  _____  _____

# My Multiple-Assignment Proofreading Record

**DIRECTIONS:** When your teacher returns a corrected writing assignment, write the title or topic on the appropriate vertical line at right. Under the topic, record the number of errors you made in each area. Use this sheet when you proofread your next assignment, taking care to check those areas in which you make frequent mistakes.

▶ **TITLE OR TOPIC OF ASSIGNMENT**

| Type of Error | | | | | | | |
|---|---|---|---|---|---|---|---|
| Sentence Fragments | | | | | | | |
| Run-on Sentences | | | | | | | |
| Subject-Verb Agreement | | | | | | | |
| Pronoun Agreement | | | | | | | |
| Incorrect Pronoun Form | | | | | | | |
| Use of Double Negative | | | | | | | |
| Comparison of Adjectives and Adverbs | | | | | | | |
| Confusing Verbs | | | | | | | |
| Irregular Verbs | | | | | | | |
| Noun Plurals and Possessives | | | | | | | |
| Capitalization | | | | | | | |
| Spelling | | | | | | | |
| End Punctuation | | | | | | | |
| Apostrophes | | | | | | | |
| Confusing Words | | | | | | | |
| Quotation Marks and Italics | | | | | | | |
| Comma or Paired Commas | | | | | | | |

# My Self-Assessment Record

| Ratings: | Needs Improvement | | Acceptable | | Excellent |
|---|---|---|---|---|---|
| | 1 | 2 | 3 | 4 | 5 |

| What I am judging (title or description) | What I like: | What I don't like: | Rating |
|---|---|---|---|
| | | | |
| | | | |
| | | | |
| | | | |
| | | | |
| | | | |
| | | | |
| | | | |
| | | | |

# Evaluating Presentation and Format

The presentation of your paper can enhance your message, making your text more accessible and pleasing to your reader. Use the following rating scale to evaluate the presentation of your own paper or a classmate's.

| **Ratings:** | Needs Improvement | | Acceptable | | Excellent |
|---|---|---|---|---|---|
| | 1 | 2 | 3 | 4 | 5 |

**Rating    Presentation Criteria**

_____  **1.** If handwritten, the slant of the letters is consistent, the letters are clearly formed, and spacing is even between words.
Comments:

_____  **2.** If word processed, there is appropriate use of boldface, italics, underlining, font and font sizes. No more than two or three different fonts are used; in addition, the font styles are used consistently.
Comments:

_____  **3.** There is a good balance between the white space on the page (spacing, margins) and the text. The intended reader can easily focus on the text; pages are not cluttered or completely filled with text.
Comments:

_____  **4.** The use of a title, subheadings, page numbers, bullets, and other features make it easy for the reader to find and understand the information presented in the paper. All headings and bullets clarify the arrangement of ideas.
Comments:

_____  **5.** All illustrations, charts, graphs, maps, tables, and other graphics work well with the text. The visuals clarify and support key points in the text.
Comments:

_____  **6.** If a Works Cited or Works Consulted list is used, the citations are complete and consistently follow the Modern Language Association (MLA) style or the style assigned by the teacher.
Comments:

**TEACHER'S REPORT**

# Progress in Writing

> **Ratings:**
>
> 1 = minimal progress      4 = more progress than expected
> 2 = less progress than expected      5 = outstanding progress
> 3 = some progress

| Volume of Writing | Rating | Comments |
|---|---|---|
| Compared with last progress report | | |
| Amount the student is writing during unscheduled school time | | |
| Amount student is writing outside of school | | |
| Writes in different genres | | |
| Writes with a variety of purposes | | |
| Writes for a variety of audiences | | |

| Writing Process | Rating | Comments |
|---|---|---|
| Has obvious purposes for writing; writes about interests and background | | |
| Demonstrates audience awareness | | |
| Plans written efforts when appropriate | | |
| Revises work | | |
| Self-assesses using his or her portfolio collection | | |

**TEACHER'S REPORT**

# Progress in Writing *(continued)*

| Writing Strategies | Rating | Comments |
|---|---|---|
| Focuses effectively on topics | | |
| Organizes material effectively | | |
| Handles details effectively | | |
| Writes with clarity and directness | | |
| Diction—uses words effectively; makes varied and purposeful choices | | |
| Appreciates the beauty and impact of language | | |
| Demonstrates variety in the development of ideas | | |
| Uses a variety of sentence structures | | |
| Is developing a personal style | | |

| Writing Mechanics | Rating | Comments |
|---|---|---|
| Uses words accurately and precisely | | |
| Follows conventions of grammar and usage | | |
| Punctuates and constructs sentences correctly | | |
| Spells correctly | | |

**TEACHER'S REPORT**

# Progress in Writing Conventions

> **Ratings:**
>
> 1 = continues to have a problem in this area
> 2 = has made gains in correcting problem
> 3 = student does this correctly

| Sentence Formation | Rating |
|---|---|
| Writes complete sentences; avoids fragments, unless used purposefully | |
| Avoids run-on sentences | |
| Avoids misplaced or dangling modifiers | |
| Uses subordination and coordination correctly in sentences; does not connect unrelated clauses | |
| Uses parallel structure | |
| Does not omit necessary words, phrases, or clauses | |
| **Usage** | **Rating** |
| Uses correct subject-verb agreement | |
| Uses tense correctly and consistently | |
| Uses auxiliary verbs and inflected verbs correctly | |
| Pronouns agree with their antecedents | |
| Pronouns are correct in nominative, possessive, and objective cases | |
| Avoids indefinite pronoun reference | |
| Uses apostrophes correctly | |
| Avoids confusion of word groups (adjectives with adverbs, singular with plural) | |
| Avoids double negatives | |
| Avoids confusion of comparative and superlative degrees | |
| Avoids inappropriate homonyms | |
| **Mechanics and Spelling** | **Rating** |
| Uses capitalization rules correctly | |
| Uses end punctuation correctly | |
| Uses internal punctuation correctly | |
| Uses and formats paragraphs appropriately | |
| Can spell common and advanced words | |

**Brief comments:**

# Creating a Guide for Evaluating Papers

Check off each step as the class completes the activity.

_____ **1.** The students read their papers aloud. No one comments until everyone has read.

_____ **2.** The students decide what the papers have in common that makes them good.

_____ **3.** The students list the four most important criteria in the form of complete sentences. Each sentence begins "A good paper has (or does) . . ."

_____ **4.** The students review the writing assignment to decide if they want to include additional criteria, and any new criteria are added to the list.

_____ **5.** Working independently, in pairs, or in peer groups, the students evaluate their papers using the criteria as a guide, indicating how successful their papers have been in achieving each goal (1 = Not at all successful, 2 = Somewhat successful, 3 = Almost totally successful, 4 = Totally successful).

As a final step, students might meet in small groups to ask peer advice on how to rewrite in order to achieve a four (4) on all criteria.

**Additional instructions or comments:**

# My Speaking and Listening Record

Use this record for both formal and informal speaking and listening experiences. Log at least one experience a week.

> **Ratings:** ✓✓✓✓ This was very important!    ✓✓ I learned a little.
>                 ✓✓✓ Worth doing/remembering     ✓ I wasted my time.

Date:

What I said, heard, or saw:

Notes about why this experience was or was not important, interesting, or useful:

Rating:

---

Date:

What I said, heard, or saw:

Notes about why this experience was or was not important, interesting, or useful:

Rating:

---

Date:

What I said, heard, or saw:

Notes about why this experience was or was not important, interesting, or useful:

Rating:

ELEMENTS OF LANGUAGE | First Course | *Assessment Alternatives*

# Inventory: Some Facts About My Speaking

| ▶ **Questions and answers about my speaking** | ▶ **More about my answers** |
|---|---|
| How do I feel about speaking to friends? | What do I like to discuss with them? |
| How do I feel about talking to adults? | Why do I feel this way? |
| How do I feel about reciting or speaking to the class? | Why do I feel this way? |
| What is the most difficult thing about speaking? | Why is it difficult? |
| What techniques have I learned to improve my speaking? | How do I use these techniques with friends or in class? |

**SELF-EVALUATION**

# Inventory: Some Facts About My Listening

| ▶ Questions and answers about my listening | ▶ More about my answers |
|---|---|
| What kinds of music do I like to listen to? | Why do I like them? |
| What TV shows and movies are my favorites? | What do I like about them? |
| How well do I listen in school? | How much do I learn by listening? |
| Do I listen carefully to what my friends say? | What do I learn from them? |
| When is it difficult for me to listen? | What makes it difficult? |
| How do I use the praise and suggestions of others to improve my skills? | How do I feel about getting praise or suggestions for improvement? |

# Evaluating My Critical Listening

To evaluate your ability to listen critically, answer the following questions about an oral presentation you recently heard. Compare your answers with those of other classmates who also heard the presentation.

**1.** What was the speaker's purpose? _____

_____

**2.** What main points did the speaker make? _____

_____

_____

**3.** What examples, details, illustrations, or facts do you remember from the presentation? _____

_____

_____

_____

**4.** Explain why you think the speaker chose to use the examples, illustrations, or other things you listed in your answer to Question 3. Be specific about as many items as you can. _____

_____

_____

_____

_____

**5.** How were the points in the presentation ordered—order of importance, logical order, or some other pattern? Was the organization effective? _____

_____

_____

_____

**6.** As the speaker spoke, were you able to draw conclusions and make predictions about what would come next? Were they accurate? Why or why not? _____

_____

_____

_____

# Evaluating My Critical Listening *(continued)*

**7.** As the speaker spoke, were you able to make connections to your own experience or prior knowledge? Why or why not? _____

_____

_____

**8.** Did you detect any bias in the speech? If so, what? _____

_____

_____

**9.** What emotional appeals or other persuasive techniques did you hear? _____

_____

_____

_____

**10.** Why do you think the speaker was or was not credible, or trustworthy, to speak on this issue?

_____

_____

**11.** If visual aids were used, were they effective? Why or why not? _____

_____

_____

**12.** What did the speaker say that puzzled or bothered you? How did this affect your reaction to the presentation? _____

_____

_____

**13.** What do you think are the strengths of the presentation? _____

_____

_____

_____

**14.** Were there any weaknesses? If so, what were they? _____

_____

_____

_____

# My Evaluation Checklist for a Speech

**Evaluation Scale:**    1 = poor/none        3 = average        5 = excellent
                         2 = fair             4 = above average

## Topic and Purpose

_____ ▪ Topic limited and manageable
_____ ▪ Specific purpose established

## Introduction

_____ ▪ Gets attention
_____ ▪ Makes purpose clear
_____ ▪ Gives needed information
_____ ▪ Relates topic to audience

## Development

_____ ▪ Main points clearly and
         logically organized
_____ ▪ Effective transitions
_____ ▪ Enough supporting evidence
_____ ▪ Evidence is relevant to
         audience and purpose
_____ ▪ Evidence clearly presented

## Conclusion

_____ ▪ Emphasizes main points
_____ ▪ Provides note of finality
_____ ▪ Ends with high interest

## Verbal Delivery

_____ ▪ Rate appropriate
_____ ▪ Volume appropriate
_____ ▪ Pronunciation correct
_____ ▪ Enunciation clear
_____ ▪ Stresses, emphasis appropriate
_____ ▪ Pauses appropriate
_____ ▪ Tone appropriate

## Nonverbal Delivery

_____ ▪ Gestures appropriate
_____ ▪ Facial expressions appropriate
_____ ▪ Eye contact good
_____ ▪ Posture acceptable
_____ ▪ Other body language
         appropriate
_____ ▪ Nervousness under control

## Use of Visual and Audio Aids

_____ ▪ Microphone handled smoothly
_____ ▪ All visual aids (videos, multimedia
         presentations, overhead transparen-
         cies, posters, slides) are clear and
         large enough for the audience to
         see
_____ ▪ All audio aids (cassette tapes, CDs,
         etc.) are clearly audible to audience
_____ ▪ All visual or audio aids enhance the
         presentation by clarifying a point or
         providing a memory aid for the audi-
         ence; none are distracting or simply
         ornamental

## Language

_____ ▪ Word choice appropriate
_____ ▪ Level of formality/informality
         appropriate to occasion

# My Evaluation of a Speech

Answer the following questions about a speech given by one of your classmates or one you heard outside of school.

**Speaker** _____ **Speech Topic** _____

- What was the speaker's purpose?

- How did the speaker's introduction get your attention?

- What main points did the speaker make?

- What evidence did the speaker give to support his or her points?

- Describe the speaker's verbal delivery. Was it effective? Why or why not?

- Describe the speaker's body language. Was it effective? Why or why not?

- Describe any visual or audio aids the speaker used. Were they effective? Why or why not?

- Was the tone of the speech appropriate for the audience, purpose, and occasion? Why or why not?

- What did you like best about this speech? Why?

- What suggestions would you give the speaker for how to improve the speech?

# Evaluating My Oral Presentation of a Literary Text

**Subject of the presentation** _____

| Questions about my oral presentation of a literary text | My responses |
|---|---|
| ■ What criteria did I use to select the text (personal interest, universal appeal, interesting theme, exciting story, etc.)? | |
| ■ Was my choice of text appropriate for my audience (subject matter, level of difficulty, length)? Why? | |
| ■ After studying the text, what interpretation did I make?  Was it valid or appropriate? Why? | |
| ■ Did I prepare an introduction that provided information about the text, its author, and any important background information? | |
| ■ Did I prepare a script of the text with cuts, notes for delivery, and marks for emphasis? | |
| ■ Did I practice my presentation?<br>■ How did this help my delivery? | |
| ■ How did I use verbal and nonverbal clues such as pitch, tone of voice, emphasis, posture, eye contact, facial expressions, and gestures to support my interpretation of the text? | |
| ■ Did my verbal and nonverbal strategies fit my purpose, audience, and occasion? Why? | |
| ■ How did I make sure that my delivery was clear and audible to everyone in my audience? | |
| ■ What did I learn from this performance that can be used to improve my next presentation? | |

# My Evaluation of an Oral Presentation of a Literary Text

**Speaker's name** _____  **Subject of presentation** _____

| Questions about the presentation | My responses |
|---|---|
| ■ Was the literature appropriate to the audience and occasion? | |
| ■ Did the speaker introduce the presentation with any background information or information about the author? | |
| ■ How did the speaker use tone of voice, pitch, gestures, and facial expression to depict different characters? | |
| ■ In what ways did the speaker use his or her own voice and tone to reflect the meaning and mood of the literary text? | |
| ■ What vocal techniques did the speaker use to emphasize the rhyme or rhythm of the text?<br>■ How did these techniques help me to appreciate the artistic qualities of the text? | |
| **Questions about my active listening** | **My responses** |
| ■ As I listened, did I try to predict what events or descriptions were coming next?<br>■ What clues enabled me to do this?<br>■ If I did not do this, how would predictions have helped my listening? | |
| ■ Did I create mental images of events or descriptions as I listened?<br>■ If so, how did this increase my understanding or appreciation?<br>■ If not, how might this have helped my listening? | |
| ■ What personal connections did I make with the text as the speaker spoke?<br>■ How did such connections help my understanding, especially of theme? | |
| ■ Was I able to make eye contact with the speaker?<br>■ What nonverbal feedback did I give to the speaker? | |

# My Evaluation of Informative Oral Presentations

**Speaker's name** _____ **Type of message** _____

| ▶ Questions about the message | ▶ My responses |
|---|---|
| ■ Was the purpose of the message clear?<br>■ Why or why not? | |
| ■ Did the message have an attention-getting introduction?<br>■ Why or why not? | |
| ■ Did the message seem appropriate to the audience's interests and level of knowledge?<br>■ Why or why not? | |
| ■ Were the main ideas or major steps easy to identify? Did they follow a logical pattern?<br>■ Why or why not? | |
| ■ Were the key points of the message supported by sufficient details and reliable data?<br>■ Why do you think so? | |
| ■ Did the message contain precise language?<br>■ Were words specific and concrete?<br>■ Was the vocabulary appropriate to the audience? | |
| ■ Were visuals or sounds used to reinforce key points of the message?<br>■ If so, were they effective? How? | |
| ■ Did the speaker seem confident?<br>■ Were the speaker's facial expressions, gestures, and movements natural? | |
| ■ What suggestions do you have for improving the message or the speaker's delivery? | |

# My Evaluation of Persuasive Oral Presentations

Speaker's name _____ Subject of presentation _____

| Questions about the message | My responses |
|---|---|
| ▪ Did the introduction grab the audience's attention?<br>▪ If so, how? | |
| ▪ Did the message seem appropriate to the interests, knowledge, and attitude of the audience? Explain. | |
| ▪ Did the speaker clearly state the specific purpose of the message?<br>▪ What was it? | |
| ▪ Were reasons and supporting evidence clearly stated?<br>▪ Did the evidence seem credible, or trustworthy?<br>▪ Why or why not? | |
| ▪ Were ethical or emotional appeals used to motivate the audience?<br>▪ Were they effective? Why or why not? | |
| ▪ Were opposing viewpoints presented and refuted with reasons and evidence?<br>▪ If so, how? | |
| ▪ Did the message contain precise language?<br>▪ Were words specific and concrete?<br>▪ Was the vocabulary appropriate to the audience? | |
| ▪ Were visuals or sounds used to reinforce key points of the message?<br>▪ If so, were they effective? How? | |
| ▪ Did the speaker seem confident and authoritative?<br>▪ Were the speaker's facial expressions, gestures, and movements natural? | |
| ▪ What suggestions do you have for improving the message or the speaker's delivery? | |

# My Evaluation of Oral Storytelling

▶ **Ratings:**

| 1 (poor) | 2 | 3 (average) | 4 | 5 (superior) |
|----------|---|-------------|---|--------------|

| ▶ EVALUATION CRITERIA | ▶ RATING | ▶ COMMENTS: Examples and explanations |
|---|---|---|
| ■ The speaker chose a story that was interesting to the intended audience. | | |
| ■ The speaker provided background information that was useful in understanding or appreciating the story. | | |
| ■ The story was told in chronological order and events built upon one another in a suspenseful way. | | |
| ■ The storyteller used formal English, except when he or she was trying to depict certain characters. | | |
| ■ The storyteller used vivid verbs and descriptive language. | | |
| ■ The storyteller used the pitch and volume of his or her voice to convey mood and to depict certain characters. | | |
| ■ The storyteller used appropriate gestures and facial expressions. | | |
| ■ The storyteller combined words and gestures effectively. | | |
| ■ The storyteller didn't include long, wordy passages that could have been more effective if acted out with gestures. | | |
| ■ The story seemed well rehearsed and smooth. | | |

# My Evaluation of a Panel Discussion

**Ratings:**

1 (poor)  2  3 (average)  4  5 (superior)

| CRITERIA FOR EVALUATION | RATING | COMMENTS: Examples and explanations |
|---|---|---|
| **Preparation**<br>■ The issue to be discussed is clearly defined.<br>■ The participants' use of relevant details and evidence shows that they have analyzed the topic (and done research, if necessary) before the panel discussion. | | |
| **Participants' speaking skills and courtesy**<br>■ Participants use an appropriate volume and tone of voice.<br>■ Participants do not interrupt one another.<br>■ Participants clearly and thoughtfully answer the questions of other participants, the moderator, and the audience. | | |
| **Participants' listening skills**<br>■ Participants ask relevant questions, use appropriate body language, and make appropriate comments to show the speaker that they are listening.<br>■ Participants take notes when others are speaking.<br>■ Participants demonstrate that they have listened to others by commenting on or summarizing the preceding speaker's response before delivering their own responses. | | |
| **Moderator's role**<br>■ The moderator introduces the discussion by providing essential information.<br>■ The moderator ensures that everyone has a chance to participate.<br>■ The moderator keeps the discussion on track.<br>■ The moderator keeps the question-and-answer session focused on brief questions and answers. | | |

# My Evaluation of a Group Discussion

▶ **Ratings:**

| 1 (poor) | 2 | 3 (average) | 4 | 5 (superior) |
|----------|---|-------------|---|--------------|

| ▶ CRITERIA FOR EVALUATION | ▶ RATING | ▶ COMMENTS: Examples and explanations |
|---------------------------|----------|---------------------------------------|
| **Purpose**<br>■ The group goal is clearly stated as a question to be answered or a problem to be solved.<br>■ Members of the group are prepared to explore the question or topic. | | |
| **Member Participation**<br>■ Each member contributes information and opinions.<br>■ Each member asks relevant questions of other members.<br>■ Members stay on task.<br>■ Members maintain eye contact with other members and speak audibly and clearly. | | |
| **Courtesy**<br>■ Members pay close attention to one another.<br>■ Members do not interrupt one another.<br>■ Members express any disagreements politely. | | |
| **Outcome**<br>■ The group produces an answer to the original question or problem.<br>■ The majority of the group members agree with the group's conclusion. | | |

**Overall evaluation**

What was the strongest contribution to the discussion? Why?

What communication skills should the group continue to work on?

# Progress in Speaking

**Ratings:**    1 = minimal progress              4 = more progress than expected
2 = less progress than expected     5 = outstanding progress
3 = some progress

| Speaking behaviors | Rating | Comments |
|---|---|---|
| Volunteers to recite in class or to contribute to class discussion | | |
| Communicates effectively with classmates one-on-one | | |
| Comments indicate keen audience awareness | | |
| Contributions are on-topic and of interest | | |
| Expresses self clearly and logically both in formal and informal speaking | | |
| Uses details effectively when speaking | | |
| Is developing effective control of voice | | |
| Can be persuasive when talking | | |
| Contributes orally to goals of smaller groups | | |

**TEACHER'S REPORT**

# Progress in Listening

| Ratings: | 1 = minimal progress | 4 = more progress than expected |
|---|---|---|
| | 2 = less progress than expected | 5 = outstanding progress |
| | 3 = some progress | |

| Listening behaviors | Rating | Comments |
|---|---|---|
| Can follow orally presented instruction | | |
| Pays attention to in-class contributions of classmates | | |
| Responds in conversation in a way that indicates comprehension | | |
| Participates in alternating exchange of ideas during conversation | | |
| Follows orally administered directions appropriately | | |
| Listens with a purpose; can ignore distractions | | |
| Can adjust type of listening (critical, reflective, empathetic, or aesthetic) to suit purpose and occasion | | |
| Is developing preferences for particular listening experiences (music, theater, etc.) | | |

**TEACHER'S REPORT**

# Progress in Oral Presentation of Literary Texts

**Ratings:**

| | |
|---|---|
| 1 = minimal progress | 4 = more progress than expected |
| 2 = less progress than expected | 5 = outstanding progress |
| 3 = some progress | |

| Presentation criteria | Rating | Comments |
|---|---|---|
| Makes appropriate selections of texts | | |
| Prepares script with cuts, marks for emphasis, and notes for delivery | | |
| Prepares an informative and appropriate introduction of the text | | |
| Practices presentation of oral interpretation | | |
| Performs a valid interpretation of the text | | |
| Uses verbal skills (pitch, tone of voice, emphasis) to communicate mood, meaning, and characterization | | |
| Uses nonverbal skills (posture, eye contact, facial expressions, gestures) to communicate mood, meaning, and characterization | | |
| Speaks clearly and audibly, with effective vocal variety | | |
| Uses suggestions from others to improve personal performances | | |

**TEACHER'S REPORT**

# Progress in Evaluation of Oral Presentations of Literary Texts

**Ratings:**

| | |
|---|---|
| 1 = minimal progress | 4 = more progress than expected |
| 2 = less progress than expected | 5 = outstanding progress |
| 3 = some progress | |

| Listening behaviors and perceptions | Rating | Comments |
|---|---|---|
| Listens to oral presentations actively | | |
| Develops appreciation for spoken language | | |
| Appreciates how nonverbal gestures and strategies enhance the spoken text | | |
| Identifies the story line in narrative texts; makes predictions about what will come next | | |
| Makes a personal connection with the literature; understands how this connection enhances his or her appreciation and understanding of literature | | |
| Interprets themes; thinks about how oral performance reveals theme, mood, and characterization | | |
| Recognizes and analyzes use of aesthetic language (figures of speech, imagery) | | |
| Discusses how use of aesthetic language enhances literary texts | | |

# Progress in Evaluating Oral Presentations of Informative and Persuasive Messages

**Ratings:**

| | |
|---|---|
| 1 = minimal progress | 4 = more progress than expected |
| 2 = less progress than expected | 5 = outstanding progress |
| 3 = some progress | |

| Listening behaviors | Rating | Comments |
|---|---|---|
| Examines the organizational structure of the message | | |
| Evaluates the support offered for the key points in the message | | |
| Examines the use of visual and audio aids in the message | | |
| Evaluates the effectiveness of the language used in the message, including the precision of explanations and/or the use of emotional appeals and other persuasive techniques | | |
| Evaluates the comprehensiveness and fairness of the message | | |
| Identifies strengths and weaknesses in the delivery of the message | | |
| Evaluates the impact of message on the intended audience | | |

# Progress in Evaluating Oral Storytelling

**Ratings:**     1 = minimal progress      4 = more progress than expected
2 = less progress than expected      5 = outstanding progress
3 = some progress

| Behaviors and perceptions | Rating | Comments |
|---|---|---|
| Evaluates whether story will interest audience | | |
| Evaluates whether background information is necessary, and, if given, whether it is adequate | | |
| Evaluates order of story's presentation and determines whether it is effective, clear, and suspenseful | | |
| Evaluates the effectiveness of the storyteller's language, including the vividness of the descriptions and action verbs | | |
| Evaluates how effectively the storyteller uses his or her voice to convey characterization and mood | | |
| Evaluates storyteller's gestures and facial expressions for appropriateness and helpfulness in telling the story | | |
| Identifies sections in the story where description might have been cut in favor of gesture and vice versa | | |
| Evaluates the smoothness of the storyteller's presentation | | |

# Progress in Evaluating Panel Discussions

**Ratings:**
1 = minimal progress
2 = less progress than expected
3 = some progress

4 = more progress than expected
5 = outstanding progress

| Behaviors and perceptions | Rating | Comments |
|---|---|---|
| Identifies the topic to be discussed | | |
| Evaluates participants' preparation for the panel discussion; notes whether they have obviously analyzed the topic or done research | | |
| Evaluates participants' volume and tone of voice for clarity and appropriateness | | |
| Evaluates participants' courtesy | | |
| Evaluates participants' attentiveness to other speakers as shown by note taking, body language, questions, and comments | | |
| Evaluates the moderator's effectiveness in ensuring that everyone has a chance to participate | | |
| Evaluates the moderator's success in keeping the discussion on track | | |

# Progress in Evaluating Group Discussions

**Ratings:**

1 = minimal progress
2 = less progress than expected
3 = some progress

4 = more progress than expected
5 = outstanding progress

| Behaviors and perceptions | Rating | Comments |
|---|---|---|
| Identifies the group goal | | |
| Evaluates whether members are prepared to explore the topic or question | | |
| Evaluates how well the group seems to stay on task | | |
| Evaluates members' contributions to the discussion; notes whether each member contributes information and asks relevant questions of other members | | |
| Evaluates whether members are engaged with the group; notes whether members maintain eye contact with one another and whether they speak audibly and clearly | | |
| Evaluates members' courtesy towards one another | | |
| Assesses whether the group reaches its goal | | |
| Assesses whether the majority of the members agree with the group's conclusion | | |

# My Viewing Record

Use this record for different types of television programs, Web sites, films, and videos. Log at least one viewing experience per week.

> **Ratings:**   ✓✓✓✓  This was very important!    ✓✓  I learned a little.
> ✓✓✓  Worth doing/remembering    ✓  I wasted my time.

---

Date:

What I saw:


Notes about why this experience was or was not important, interesting, or useful:


Rating:

---

Date:

What I saw:


Notes about why this experience was or was not important, interesting, or useful:


Rating:

---

Date:

What I saw:


Notes about why this experience was or was not important, interesting, or useful:


Rating:

**SELF-EVALUATION**

# Inventory: Some Questions and Answers About My Viewing

| ▶ Questions and answers about my viewing | ▶ More about my answers |
|---|---|
| What kinds of visual media do I use or prefer—television, film, Web, or another type? | What do I like about these kinds of media? |
| What kinds of television shows and movies do I prefer? | Why do I like them the best? |
| How much am I influenced by what I see? For example, how apt am I to purchase something I have seen advertised? | What associations do I make between the image I see and myself? What emotions do I think advertising plays on? |
| Who makes the TV shows, magazines, or videos I like best? | What do I think is the purpose of these programs, magazines, or videos? |
| Who is the target audience of the shows and other media I like? How do I know? | How would people outside this target audience interpret these shows or other media? |
| Do I evaluate visual or audio techniques (close shots, objects out of focus, music, voice-overs, etc.)? | How aware of these techniques am I as I watch? |

# Inventory: Some Questions and Answers About My Representing

| Questions and answers about my representing | More about my answers |
|---|---|
| What visual media do I like to use—videos, Web, painting, drawing, or another form? | What do I like about using these visual media? |
| Before beginning any project, do I think about which visual medium would best suit my purpose? | How do visual media differ? What are their individual strengths and weaknesses? |
| Do I continually consider my audience when creating visual media? | How do my final products show that I've thought about audience? |
| Do I consider design elements such as color, line, graphics, images, and photos when using visual media? | How and why do I use design elements? |
| Do I think about how a viewer or reader will navigate through the visual media I make—particularly Web sites? | How do I make sure that my information is complete without being cluttered or disorganized? |
| When using film or video, do I consider how the sound and picture will work together? | How do I make sure that the sound and images in my film or video complement each other? |

# My Evaluation of Multimedia Presentations

**Ratings:**

1 (poor)    2    3 (average)    4    5 (superior)

| CRITERIA FOR EVALUATION | RATING | COMMENTS: Examples and explanations |
|---|---|---|
| **Content**<br>■ The presenter states the purpose of the presentation at the beginning.<br>■ The presentation is interesting and informative.<br>■ The presentation is organized in an effective way. | | |
| **Delivery**<br>■ The presenter speaks clearly and loudly enough to be heard by the entire audience.<br>■ The speaker gives the audience enough time to look at each visual.<br>■ The speaker faces the audience during most of the presentation, only looking away when pointing out something on the computer or video screen.<br>■ The speaker operates all equipment smoothly. | | |
| **Visuals**<br>■ The visuals present essential and relevant information.<br>■ The speaker presents the visuals at the same time as the points they reinforce.<br>■ Charts, graphs, and photos are easy to read and understand.<br>■ Charts and graphs use color or design elements to make the information clearer. | | |
| **Music/sound effects**<br>■ The music sets a mood.<br>■ The sound effects match the images.<br>■ The music or sound effects are not distracting. | | |

# My Evaluation of a Documentary

**DIRECTIONS:** Circle the number in each row below to indicate your evaluation of each item.

> **Ratings:**
>
> 1 = Poorly done  4 = Good
> 2 = Has some flaws  5 = Superior
> 3 = Average

## I.  CONTENT

| | |
|---|---|
| The documentary reveals a main idea. | 1  2  3  4  5 |
| The documentary is interesting. | 1  2  3  4  5 |
| The documentary contributes to the viewer's understanding of the topic. | 1  2  3  4  5 |
| The documentary provides a variety of content—images of the narrator, interviews, action sequences, graphs, still photos, and so on. | 1  2  3  4  5 |
| The documentary presents its subject accurately and fairly. | 1  2  3  4  5 |

## II.  ORGANIZATION

| | |
|---|---|
| The beginning of the documentary introduces the subject and grabs your attention. | 1  2  3  4  5 |
| Each scene gives new information. | 1  2  3  4  5 |
| The sequence of scenes makes sense; if appropriate, the sequence of shots builds suspense. | 1  2  3  4  5 |
| The voice-over fits with the action and dialogue. | 1  2  3  4  5 |
| The end of the documentary sums up the information presented and leaves you with a final impression. | 1  2  3  4  5 |

## III.  TECHNICAL QUALITY

| | |
|---|---|
| The sound quality is audible and consistent. | 1  2  3  4  5 |
| The music adds atmosphere without distracting from the action or dialogue. | 1  2  3  4  5 |
| The camera angles are clear and interesting. | 1  2  3  4  5 |
| The combination of camera shots is smooth; transitions are used effectively between shots. | 1  2  3  4  5 |
| Lighting is used to enhance atmosphere. | 1  2  3  4  5 |

**Overall Evaluation or Comments:**

# My Evaluation of a Newspaper

Choose a school, local, or national newspaper and answer the following questions.

**1.** Who is the intended audience for the newspaper? Why do you think so?

**2.** Is there a mix of stories and features in the paper, including hard-hitting news stories, human interest stories, editorials, and so on? What kinds of stories take up the most space?

**3.** How well organized is the layout? Are photos mixed in with the text? Are story headlines presented and arranged in an appealing way?

**4.** What kind of visuals are used? What purpose do they seem to have?

**5.** Choose a particular story on the front page, and state the story's main idea.

**6.** In the particular story you chose, look for quotations. Why are these people's words used in the story?

**7.** Ask yourself how the *5W-How?* questions (*who? what? where? when? why?* and *how?*) are answered in the story. If these questions aren't answered, why not?

**8.** Do you think the newspaper is informative and fair? Why or why not?

# My Evaluation of a Photograph

Choose a photograph from a newspaper story and answer the following questions.

**1.** Describe what the photo portrays.

**2.** From what camera angle is the photo taken—from above, below, or some other angle?

**3.** Explain the effect of the camera angle on your response to the photo. Does it make the subject look fragile, intimidating, or something else?

**4.** How is the photo cropped? What do you suspect might be just outside the frame of the photo?

**5.** Would you react differently to the photo if you could see more of the scene or if the photo was a tighter close-up? Explain your answer.

**6.** Does the photo's caption give you just factual information, or does it show a positive or negative view of the photo? Explain your answer.

**7.** What other caption could you give the photo? How might that caption change how viewers respond to the photo?

**8.** How does the photo make you feel? Does it invite an emotional reaction? Explain.

**9.** How does the photo contribute to the text of the story? Does it convey important information?

# My Evaluation of a Television News Program

View a news program and take notes. Then, answer the following questions.

1. Name the news program you are evaluating. Is it a national news program, a local news program, or a newsmagazine? Who do you think is its primary audience?

2. Name some of the stories presented and then explain why you think they were shown. Did they meet the common news criteria of timeliness, serious impact on the audience, human interest, or news about celebrities?

3. Choose a particular news story and explain how it captures the viewer's attention. Do its words or images play upon the viewer's emotions? If so, how?

4. Whose points of view are represented in the story? Whose are left out? Why?

5. Who reports the news? Do reporters in the field and outside experts interact with the anchors or not? Why do you think this is (or is not) done?

6. What do the program's set, slogan, title logo, and opening music tell you about its tone and purpose?

7. What advertisements are shown in the commercials that interrupt the show? Why do you think they are the ones used?

8. How reliable do you think this news program is? Why do you think so?

# My Comparison of Media: Film and Literature

Use this form to evaluate and compare a story or book and its TV or film version.

**1.** What are the names of the story or book and the TV or film adaptation of the story?

**2.** What genre do the story or book and its adaptation belong to—science fiction, animal stories, mysteries, Westerns, or another genre? What are the characteristics of this genre?

**3.** How does the TV or film version represent the plot of the story or book? Does it add events or leave them out? Why?

**4.** How does the TV or film version depict the main characters of the book? If there are significant changes, what are they and why do you think they were made?

**5.** How well does the TV or film version use dialogue to tell the story or convey the emotions of the characters? Is the dialogue faithful to the book or story? Why or why not?

**6.** How do the actors in the TV or film version use facial expressions and body movements to convey what the characters feel?

**7.** What camera techniques (close-ups, long shots) does the film use to tell the story or convey the characters' emotions? Are they effective?

**8.** What is your overall evaluation of the TV or film version of the book or story? How does it compare to the printed text? Explain your answer.

# My Evaluation of a Television Entertainment Program

View a television sitcom or drama and take notes. Then, answer the following questions.

**1.** What is the name of the show?

**2.** What is the show's genre—drama, sitcom, or some other type of program? What are the characteristics of that type of program?

**3.** What audience do you think it targets? Why do you think so?

**4.** What is the main plot of the show? Is it realistic? Why or why not?

**5.** What is the main setting of the show? Is it realistic? Why or why not?

**6.** Who are the main characters on the show? Are they realistic, or "round," characters—or are they stereotypes? What makes you think so?

**7.** How do you respond to the characters? Do you identify with them? Why or why not?

**8.** What is the theme of the show? Why do you think so?

**9.** What is your overall assessment of the show? Why?

# My Evaluation of Graphics

**DIRECTIONS:** Circle a number in each row below to indicate your evaluation of each item.

| **Ratings:** | 1 = Poorly done | 4 = Good |
| --- | --- | --- |
| | 2 = Has some flaws | 5 = Superior |
| | 3 = Average | |

## I. PLANNING

- The graphic is an appropriate way to communicate the information.    1  2  3  4  5

- The graphic gives enough information to make the process or results clearly understandable, but not so much information that the graphic is cluttered or distracting.    1  2  3  4  5

- The graphic supports a point made in the essay, article, or presentation.    1  2  3  4  5

## II. LABELS

- The graphic has a clear title or caption.    1  2  3  4  5

- Labels are accurate and complete but not wordy.    1  2  3  4  5

- The graphic has a clear key or legend.    1  2  3  4  5

- If the information represented was found in a research source, the source is clearly identified.    1  2  3  4  5

## III. DESIGN AND SPATIAL ORGANIZATION

- If color is used, it is limited to just a few colors that are used consistently.    1  2  3  4  5

- The movement in a flowchart is clear; arrows direct the reader's eye in a logical pattern.    1  2  3  4  5

- The vertical and horizontal axes of a bar or line graph are clearly identified, so the reader can tell what is being measured and what measurements are being used.    1  2  3  4  5

- The wedges of a pie chart are labeled and arranged in a logical way.    1  2  3  4  5

- Charts and tables have easily identifiable categories listed at the top.    1  2  3  4  5

- Time lines clearly show events from left to right.    1  2  3  4  5

**Overall Evaluation:**

# My Evaluation of a Television Commercial

Use this form to evaluate a television commercial. If possible, tape the commercial so you can watch it a number of times during your evaluation.

**1.** What is the product or service being advertised?

**2.** Who made the ad and why?

**3.** Who is the target audience of the ad? Why do you think so?

**4.** Describe who or what is featured in the ad. Why are these people or things shown?

**5.** What is the setting of the ad? Why is this setting used?

**6.** Do you detect any persuasive techniques, such as bandwagon, snob appeal, and so on? Why are they effective (or ineffective)?

**7.** Does the ad have a plot or story? If so, how does it contribute to the ad's message?

**8.** How does music or sound contribute to the ad's message or appeal to the target audience?

**9.** How do camera angles contribute to the ad's message or appeal to the ad's target audience?

**10.** Does the ad appeal to your emotions, logic, or ethics? If so, how and why?

**11.** What show were you watching when you saw the ad? What does that show tell you about the purpose and target audience of the ad?

**12.** Is the ad effective? Why or why not?

# My Evaluation of a Print Advertisement

Use this form to evaluate an advertisement from a newspaper or magazine.

**1.** What is the message of the ad?

**2.** Who made the ad and why?

**3.** Who is the target audience of the ad? Why do you think so?

**4.** Does the ad appeal to the reader's intellect by presenting valid, logical reasons? If so, what are they?

**5.** Does the ad use persuasive techniques (bandwagon, testimonial, plain folks, loaded words, and so on) to appeal to the reader's emotions and desires? What techniques does it use and why are they effective (or ineffective)?

**6.** Does the ad use images to effectively appeal to the reader's emotions or senses? What are they? Why are they effective (or ineffective)?

**7.** How does the ad use color, line, shape, texture, or camera angle to catch the reader's attention and reinforce the message?

**8.** Does the ad have a catchy slogan? Is the slogan appropriate for the target audience? Explain.

**9.** Does the ad accurately represent its product, service, idea, or cause? Why or why not?

**10**. How effective is the ad? Why?

# My Evaluation of a Web Site

**Ratings:**

| 1 (poor) | 2 | 3 (average) | 4 | 5 (superior) |

| CRITERIA FOR EVALUATION | RATING | COMMENTS: Examples and explanations |
|---|---|---|
| **Clarity**<br>■ The site is easy to navigate.<br>■ The site contains a clear index.<br>■ Hyperlinks are clearly distinguished from text.<br>■ Text is easy to read. | | |
| **Content**<br>■ The site contains complete information.<br>■ The site is objective or makes an effort to present both sides of an issue.<br>■ The site's producer is clearly identified on the home page.<br>■ The site is authoritative; the site and its producer seem to be trustworthy sources of information.<br>■ The content is current; the last revision date on the page is reasonably recent. | | |
| **Design**<br>■ Color is used effectively—one color is used consistently for each different element of the site (hyperlinks, headings, etc.).<br>■ Photos, graphics, or animation enhance the site without distracting the viewer.<br>■ Visuals download quickly. | | |
| **Organization**<br>■ All closely related information is located on a single page.<br>■ The pages are not crowded with too much text.<br>■ The information is organized in a logical way. | | |

**TEACHER'S REPORT**

# Progress in Viewing

> **Ratings:**     1 = minimal progress              4 = more progress than expected
>                  2 = less progress than expected   5 = outstanding progress
>                  3 = some progress

| Viewing perceptions and behaviors | Rating | Comments |
|---|---|---|
| Identifies the purpose of various media presentations (i.e., informative, advertising, entertainment shows) | | |
| Analyzes credibility of programs viewed (who made it and why) | | |
| Speculates about the target audience of a media message and identifies what techniques are used to address that audience | | |
| Analyzes own response to different kinds of media messages | | |
| Evaluates audio and visual techniques (special effects, camera angles, music, etc.) and their effects | | |
| Draws conclusions and forms opinions about the purpose and effects of media messages | | |
| Articulates reasons for personal preferences in TV and movie viewing | | |

# Progress in Representing

| Ratings: | 1 = minimal progress | 4 = more progress than expected |
| --- | --- | --- |
| | 2 = less progress than expected | 5 = outstanding progress |
| | 3 = some progress | |

| Representing behaviors and perceptions | Rating | Comments |
| --- | --- | --- |
| Chooses medium appropriate to his or her purpose | | |
| Considers target audience and how to attract its members | | |
| Provides accurate, complete information without disorganization or clutter | | |
| Uses color, line, graphics, images, and photos to attract attention and provide clear information | | |
| Considers how a viewer or reader will navigate through the media product; the design of product reflects thinking about the ease of its use | | |
| If the product is a film or video, uses sound and images to complement each other; product reflects student's awareness of effective expository or storytelling techniques | | |
| Reflects on the strengths and weaknesses of the final product | | |

**TEACHER'S REPORT**

# Progress in Evaluating Multimedia Presentations

> **Ratings:**
>
> 1 = minimal progress          4 = more progress than expected
>
> 2 = less progress than expected     5 = outstanding progress
>
> 3 = some progress

| Behaviors and perceptions | Rating | Comments |
|---|---|---|
| Identifies the purpose of the presentation | | |
| Evaluates whether the presentation is informative and interesting | | |
| Evaluates how well the visuals support the purpose of the presentation; can detect whether they are irrelevant or used solely for ornamentation | | |
| Evaluates the clarity of the visuals | | |
| Evaluates the organization of the presentation | | |
| Evaluates the effectiveness and relevance of the music and/or sound effects | | |
| Evaluates the presenter's delivery | | |

# Progress in Evaluating Documentaries

| Ratings: | 1 = minimal progress | 4 = more progress than expected |
|---|---|---|
| | 2 = less progress than expected | 5 = outstanding progress |
| | 3 = some progress | |

| Behaviors and perceptions | Rating | Comments |
|---|---|---|
| Identifies the topic and overall purpose of the documentary | | |
| Evaluates the documentary's camera work and editing; identifies the purpose or intended effect of certain shots and edits | | |
| Evaluates the documentary's use of music and sound effects; assesses how well sound and image complement each other | | |
| Evaluates the documentary's organization; assesses whether the sequences and transitions make sense and create interest | | |
| Evaluates the documentary's use of lighting to create mood and to portray scenes clearly | | |
| Evaluates the documentary's point of view and fairness | | |
| Evaluates the documentary's thoroughness; can cite details that reveal the maker's knowledge and/or research | | |
| Assesses the informativeness and entertainment value of the documentary | | |

# Progress in Evaluating Newspapers

**Ratings:**
1 = minimal progress
2 = less progress than expected
3 = some progress

4 = more progress than expected
5 = outstanding progress

| Behaviors and perceptions | Rating | Comments |
|---|---|---|
| Speculates about the newspaper's intended audience | | |
| Evaluates the mix of stories in the paper and identifies which type of stories are most prominent | | |
| Evaluates the design of the paper, including layout, fonts, and placement of text and images | | |
| Evaluates visuals and their effects and purposes | | |
| Can identify emotional appeals and shows awareness of why they are used in stories and photos | | |
| Identifies quotations in a particular story and evaluates whether they are from appropriate and authoritative sources | | |
| Can evaluate whether a particular news story answers the *5W-H?* questions and, if not, can speculate about why not | | |

# Progress in Evaluating Photographs

▶ **Ratings:**
| | |
|---|---|
| 1 = minimal progress | 4 = more progress than expected |
| 2 = less progress than expected | 5 = outstanding progress |
| 3 = some progress | |

| ▶ Behaviors and perceptions | ▶ Rating | ▶ Comments |
|---|---|---|
| Can describe photo in detail | | |
| Can identify the angle from which the photo is taken and what effect that angle has on the viewer's response | | |
| Can tell how photo is cropped or speculate about what lies outside the photo's frame | | |
| Can assess the effect of cropping on the viewer's response to the photo | | |
| Can evaluate the tone and purpose of the caption | | |
| Can identify how the caption affects the viewer's response to the photo | | |
| Can assess how the photo makes him or her feel about the subject of the photo | | |
| Can assess how the photo contributes to the text of the news story | | |
| Can assess the photo's effectiveness in conveying information | | |
| Can give specific and relevant reasons for his or her answers | | |

**TEACHER'S REPORT**

# Progress in Evaluating Television News

**Ratings:**　　　1 = minimal progress　　　　　　　4 = more progress than expected
　　　　　　　　　2 = less progress than expected　　5 = outstanding progress
　　　　　　　　　3 = some progress

| Behaviors and perceptions | Rating | Comments |
|---|---|---|
| Can identify the genre of the news program and identify some of its characteristics | | |
| Can identify the criteria the news program's producers might have used in choosing individual stories | | |
| Can speculate about target audience and offer support for his or her ideas | | |
| Evaluates fairness of stories; notes whose point of view is adopted and whose is omitted | | |
| Evaluates visuals and their possible emotional impact | | |
| Assesses the show's anchors, set, slogan, and music; notes how all elements contribute to the purpose and tone of the show | | |
| Assesses what information the interrupting advertisements can provide about the audience and purpose of the show | | |
| Evaluates the overall reliability of the show and provides support for opinion | | |

**TEACHER'S REPORT**

# Progress in Evaluating Film and TV Entertainment Genres

▶ **Ratings:**

1 = minimal progress
2 = less progress than expected
3 = some progress

4 = more progress than expected
5 = outstanding progress

| Behaviors and perceptions | ▶ Rating | ▶ Comments |
|---|---|---|
| Student identifies genre of show or film and can recall several characteristics of that genre | | |
| Can thoughtfully speculate about target audience | | |
| Evaluates setting | | |
| Evaluates characters and dialogue; can distinguish complex characterization from stereotypes | | |
| Evaluates plot | | |
| Identifies theme and can provide support for answer | | |
| If film or show is an adaptation of a literary work, can evaluate how well the actors, script, setting, and camera techniques capture the style and meaning of the text | | |
| If film or show is an adaptation of a literary work, can speculate about why any changes in character, plot, or setting were made | | |
| Can offer an overall assessment and provide support for this opinion | | |

# Progress in Evaluating Graphics

> **Ratings:**     1 = minimal progress        4 = more progress than expected
> 2 = less progress than expected     5 = outstanding progress
> 3 = some progress

| ▶ Behaviors and perceptions | ▶ Rating | ▶ Comments |
|---|---|---|
| Evaluates the suitability of the graphic to convey the information it contains and the graphic's relevance to the text it supports | | |
| Evaluates the completeness and clarity of the graphic; checks that the graphic is not cluttered with too much information | | |
| Evaluates the completeness and clarity of the graphic's labels | | |
| Identifies the graphic's key or legend and evaluates its clarity | | |
| Evaluates the use of color for helpfulness and consistency | | |
| Evaluates the logic and organization of charts, tables, flowcharts, graphs, and time lines | | |
| Can support evaluations with clear reasons | | |

**TEACHER'S REPORT**

# Progress in Evaluating Advertising

**Ratings:**

| | |
|---|---|
| 1 = minimal progress | 4 = more progress than expected |
| 2 = less progress than expected | 5 = outstanding progress |
| 3 = some progress | |

| Behaviors and perceptions | Rating | Comments |
|---|---|---|
| Identifies the purpose and target audience of the ad | | |
| Evaluates the ad's slogan, written copy, voice-over, dialogue, or music for clarity, interest, and appropriateness for the target audience | | |
| Identifies logical or ethical appeals in the ad | | |
| Identifies persuasive techniques and emotional appeals and evaluates their effects | | |
| Evaluates the ad's selection of images and use of color, line, texture, and camera angles | | |
| Evaluates a television ad's use of characters and plot and speculates about the intended purpose and effect of these elements | | |
| Evaluates the fairness of the ad | | |
| Provides thoughtful reasons and concrete evidence for all evaluations | | |

# Progress in Evaluating Web Sites

| Ratings: | 1 = minimal progress | 4 = more progress than expected |
|---|---|---|
| | 2 = less progress than expected | 5 = outstanding progress |
| | 3 = some progress | |

| Behaviors and perceptions | Rating | Comments |
|---|---|---|
| Evaluates the site's ease of navigation and the logic of its organization | | |
| Evaluates the accuracy and objectivity of the site's information | | |
| Identifies the site's producer and assesses his or her credibility | | |
| Evaluates whether the site is current | | |
| Evaluates the site's use of images, graphics, photos, and animation | | |
| Evaluates the site's use of color for consistency and helpfulness | | |
| Evaluates the site's overall design for clarity and absence of clutter | | |

# My Cooperative Learning Record

Use this record to track and evaluate your conferences with peer partners, your discussions in small groups, your group projects, and your teacher conferences.

> **Ratings:** ✓✓✓✓ This was very important!    ✓✓ I learned a little.
> ✓✓✓ Worth doing/remembering    ✓ I wasted my time.

---

Date:

What I said, heard, or learned:

Notes about why this experience was or was not important, interesting, or useful:

Rating:

---

Date:

What I said, heard, or learned:

Notes about why this experience was or was not important, interesting, or useful:

Rating:

---

Date:

What I said, heard, or learned:

Notes about why this experience was or was not important, interesting, or useful:

Rating:

# Inventory: Some Questions and Answers About My Cooperative Learning

| ▶ Questions and answers about cooperative learning | ▶ More about my answers |
|---|---|
| How do I feel about my role in the group? | What do I feel this way? |
| How much responsibility do I assume? | Do I like doing this? Why or why not? |
| How much do I participate in the group? | What do others learn from me? |
| How well do I stay on task? | What do I learn from others? |
| What is the most difficult thing about cooperative learning? | Why is it difficult? |
| What do I like about working cooperatively with others? | How might I use cooperative learning skills outside of school? |

# Evaluation of My Cooperative Learning

Use these questions to consider and evaluate your contributions to group activities.

**1.** What was your role in the group?

_____

**2.** What did you need to do to be useful in that role?

_____

_____

_____

_____

**3.** Were you attentive and respectful to others in the group? What did you do to show these things?

_____

_____

_____

_____

**4.** Were you able to stick to the subject or project at hand? Why or why not?

_____

_____

_____

_____

**5.** What was your most important contribution to the group?

_____

_____

_____

_____

**6.** What could you do to become a more effective group member?

_____

_____

_____

_____

# My Evaluation of Cooperative Learning

Use these questions to evaluate the contributions of another student in your group.

**Group member's name:** _____  **Group member's role in the group:** _____

**1.** Three words I would use to describe how the group member performed the role are

_____

**2.** The member did the following things to work well with others (for example, asked questions to clarify the task, organized the agenda, or showed courtesy to other members):

_____

_____

_____

_____

_____

**3.** The most important contribution the member made to the group was _____

_____

_____

_____

_____

_____

**4.** This contribution was important to the group because _____

_____

_____

_____

_____

**5.** The group member could contribute more to the group if he or she _____

_____

_____

_____

_____

# My Evaluation of Group Participation

Think about the work your small group did and then answer the following questions.

**1.** The students who participated in this group were _____

_____

_____

**2.** Our task was _____

_____

_____

_____

**3.** ▶ Circle your response to the following statements.

    1 = Strongly Disagree    2 = Disagree Somewhat    3 = Agree    4 = Strongly Agree

| | | | | |
|---|---|---|---|---|
| The group did a good job of staying on task. | 1 | 2 | 3 | 4 |
| Every member of the group contributed to the group. | 1 | 2 | 3 | 4 |
| Each member of the group treated the other members of the group with respect and kindness. | 1 | 2 | 3 | 4 |
| The group felt that the task was worth accomplishing. | 1 | 2 | 3 | 4 |
| Each member of the group learned something from this experience. | 1 | 2 | 3 | 4 |

**4.** What is the group's greatest strength? _____

_____

_____

_____

_____

_____

**5.** What does this group need to do to become more productive? _____

_____

_____

_____

_____

_____

**TEACHER'S REPORT**

# Progress in Cooperative Learning

**Ratings:**

| | |
|---|---|
| 1 = minimal progress | 4 = more progress than expected |
| 2 = less progress than expected | 5 = outstanding progress |
| 3 = some progress | |

| Behaviors and perceptions | Rating | Comments |
|---|---|---|
| Actively participates in assigned role | | |
| Communicates effectively with the group | | |
| Assumes individual responsibility in learning | | |
| Organizes work | | |
| Focuses effectively on topic | | |
| Demonstrates multiple problem-solving strategies | | |
| Respects opinions, strengths, and weaknesses of others in group | | |
| Demonstrates a positive attitude with the group | | |
| Encourages others to participate | | |
| Explains concepts; paraphrases and summarizes ideas | | |
| Adds ideas and offers input | | |
| Completes work | | |

# Holistic Scale: Six Points

**Score: 6** | **A score "6" paper has the following characteristics.**

All parts of the prompt are addressed with insight and control, and the writing is focused, clear, and well developed. All support is ample, specific, and relevant. The paper's organizational pattern enables a logical, coherent progression of ideas. The writer's engagement with the topic is clearly evident, as is his or her consideration of the intended audience's interest in and knowledge of the topic. The writer makes controlled and effective word choices and uses a natural, fresh voice; the paper is free of clichés and wooden phrasing. Sentence structure is varied, and fragments are used only when appropriate to the writer's purpose. There are very few, if any, convention errors in mechanics, usage, and punctuation.

**Score: 5** | **A score "5" paper has the following characteristics.**

The paper addresses all parts of the prompt with some degree of clarity and insight, although some minor lapses in coherence may be evident. The writer shows a consideration of purpose and audience, and the paper's organizational pattern is clear. All support is sufficient, specific, and relevant. When causal relationships are discussed, the writer makes all connections clear and explicit. The paper also exhibits a good command of language, including accurate and descriptive word choices. Sentence structure is varied and sentences are complete except when fragments are used for effect. The writer makes few errors in mechanics, usage, and spelling.

**Score: 4** | **A score "4" paper has the following characteristics.**

For the most part, the paper is focused on the topic but may include irrelevant or loosely related material. The writer uses an appropriate organizational pattern, although some confusion in the logical progression of ideas may occur. The support includes specific details and precise word choices but is not ample nor evenly elaborated. In some responses, the writer demonstrates an awareness of audience, although this awareness is not exhibited consistently throughout the paper. Most sentences are complete, but there is little variation in sentence structure. There are few egregious errors in grammar, usage, and spelling.

**Score: 3** | **A score "3" paper has the following characteristics.**

The paper addresses the topic in a reasonably focused way but may include irrelevant or loosely related material. The writer attempts to follow an organizational pattern, but may lapse into digressions or fail to provide transitions between ideas. The paper may also demonstrate little awareness of or connec-

# Holistic Scale: Six Points *(continued)*

tion to an audience. Some support, which may include specific details and relevant examples, is included, but development of such support is not consistent or substantial. Some "3" papers may appear to be somewhat elaborated summaries or lists of ideas. The writer's choice of words is generally adequate, but may be predictable or imprecise. The writer may vary his or her sentence structure very little, or not at all. Usually, however, the writer has a command of the conventions of written language.

**Score: 2**

**A score "2" paper has the following characteristics.**
The paper is generally responsive to the prompt but includes irrelevant or loosely related material. The paper may show few signs of an overall organizational strategy and few explicit transitions between ideas. Some papers may not exhibit a logical relationship between the main idea and subordinate ideas. Others may have an initial sense of purpose but then veer off-track. Support is generally unelaborated, consisting of lists or simple summary. The writer's choice of words is often imprecise or inappropriate, and sentence structure is unvaried or faulty. The writer may show limited knowledge of basic writing conventions.

**Score: 1**

**A score "1" paper has the following characteristics.**
The paper may address the prompt in only a minimal or tangential way. In addition, the paper may be highly fragmentary, often a listing of ideas with little development or organization of support. If any attempt to support or organize ideas is exhibited, a "1" paper is too short or skeletal to achieve a higher score. There is often no sense of audience or audience is badly misperceived. Inappropriate word choice or frequent errors in sentence structure and usage may also completely hinder the paper's readability. The writer may make blatant errors in grammar, usage, and mechanics.

**Unscorable**

**The paper is unscorable because**
- the response is not relevant to the prompt.
- the response is only a rewording of the prompt.
- the response contains an insufficient amount of writing to determine if it addresses the prompt.
- the response is a copy of a previously published work.
- the response is illegible, incomprehensible, or blank.

# Holistic Scale: Six Points

**Score: 6** | **A score "6" paper has the following characteristics.**

All parts of the prompt are addressed with insight and control, and the writing is focused, well developed, and forceful in arguing the writer's position. The writer maintains a consistent position throughout, and rebuts counterarguments with skill and purpose. All support is specific, relevant, and persuasive. The paper's organizational pattern demonstrates an awareness of the relative strength of the paper's arguments, ordering them in an obviously persuasive way. The paper also demonstrates the writer's engagement with the issue and his or her consideration of the readers' opinions and preconceptions about the issue. The writer makes controlled and effective word choices and uses a natural, fresh voice. Sentence structure is varied and fragments are only used when appropriate to the writer's purpose. There are very few, if any, errors in grammar, usage, and mechanics.

**Score: 5** | **A score "5" paper has the following characteristics.**

The paper addresses all parts of the prompt with insight and attention to the persuasive task, although some minor lapses in coherence may be evident. The writer shows that he or she understands fundamental persuasive strategies and has considered audience, occasion, and tone. The paper's organizational pattern is clear and all support is sufficient, specific, relevant, and persuasive. The paper also exhibits a command of language, including precise, forceful, and vivid word choices. Sentence structure is varied and sentences are complete except when fragments are used for effect. The writer makes few errors in mechanics, usage, and spelling.

**Score: 4** | **A score "4" paper has the following characteristics.**

For the most part, the paper is focused on the persuasive task but may include some irrelevant or loosely related material. The writer uses an appropriate organizational pattern, although the persuasiveness of the argument may be undercut by occasional lapses in logic or coherence. The paper's support includes specific details, relevant examples, and precise word choices but is not ample nor evenly elaborated. In some responses, the writer demonstrates an awareness of audience, although this awareness may not be exhibited consistently throughout the paper. Most sentences are complete, but there is little variation in sentence structure. There are few egregious errors in mechanics, usage, and grammar.

**Score: 3** | **A score "3" paper has the following characteristics.**

The paper addresses the persuasive task in a reasonably

# Holistic Scale: Six Points (continued)

focused way but may include irrelevant or loosely related material. The writer attempts to follow an organizational pattern, but may lapse into digressions or fail to provide transitions between ideas. The paper may also demonstrate little awareness of audience. Some support, which may include specific details and relevant examples, is included, but development of such support is not consistent or substantial. The writer's choice of words is generally adequate, but may be predictable or imprecise. The writer may vary his or her sentence structure very little, or not at all. Usually, however, the writer shows a command of the conventions of grammar, mechanics, and usage.

**Score: 2**

**A score "2" paper has the following characteristics.**

The paper is generally responsive to the prompt but includes irrelevant or loosely related material. Many "2" papers will not offer a clear position on the issue nor pursue an explicitly persuasive strategy. The paper may show few signs of an overall organizational strategy and few clear transitions between ideas. Some papers may have an initial sense of purpose but then veer off-track. Support is generally unelaborated, consisting of lists or simple summary. The writer's choice of words is often imprecise or inappropriate, and sentence structure is unvaried or faulty. The writer may show limited knowledge of the basic conventions of written language.

**Score: 1**

**A score "1" paper has the following characteristics.**

The paper may only address the prompt in a minimal or tangential way. In addition, the paper may be highly fragmentary, often a listing of ideas with little development of support. Frequently, no organizational pattern is apparent. If any attempt to support or organize ideas is exhibited, a "1" paper is too short or skeletal to achieve a higher score. There is often no sense of audience or audience is badly misperceived. Inappropriate word choice and frequent errors in sentence structure and usage may also completely hinder the paper's readability. The writer may make blatant errors in mechanics, usage, and grammar.

**Unscorable**

**The paper is unscorable because**

- the response is not relevant to the prompt.
- the response is only a rewording of the prompt.
- the response contains an insufficient amount of writing to determine if it addresses the prompt.
- the response is a copy of a previously published work.
- the response is illegible, incomprehensible, or blank.

# Holistic Scale: Six Points

**Score: 6** | **A score "6" paper has the following characteristics.**

All parts of the prompt are addressed with insight and control, and the writing is focused, well developed, and forceful. The writer presents a clear recommendation based on thoughtful criteria. All support is specific, relevant, and persuasive. The paper's organizational pattern enables a logical progression of ideas. The paper also demonstrates the writer's engagement with the issue and his or her consideration of the audience. The writer makes controlled and effective word choices and reveals a natural, fresh voice. Sentence structure is varied and there are very few errors in mechanics, usage, and grammar. The response is written in a conventional letter format.

**Score: 5** | **A score "5" paper has the following characteristics.**

The paper addresses all parts of the prompt with insight, although some minor lapses in coherence may be evident. The writer shows that he or she understands the criteria that might be applied to a book, including literary concepts, and has considered audience. The paper's organizational pattern is clear and all support is sufficient, specific, relevant, and persuasive. The paper also exhibits a good command of language, including precise, forceful, and vivid word choices. Sentence structure is varied and the writer makes few errors in mechanics, usage, and grammar. Letter format is used, although it may not match a conventional format.

**Score: 4** | **A score "4" paper has the following characteristics.**

For the most part, the paper is focused on the evaluative task but may include some irrelevant or loosely related material. The writer uses an appropriate organizational pattern, although there may be occasional lapses in logic or coherence. The paper's support includes specific details, relevant examples, and precise word choices but is not ample nor evenly elaborated. In some responses, the writer demonstrates an awareness of audience, although this awareness may not be exhibited consistently throughout the paper. Most sentences are complete, but there is little variation in sentence structure. There are few egregious errors in mechanics, usage, and spelling. Letter format may be missing except for a greeting and/or closing.

**Score: 3** | **A score "3" paper has the following characteristics.**

The paper addresses the evaluative task in a reasonably focused way but may include irrelevant or loosely related material. The writer attempts to follow an organizational pattern, but may lapse into digressions or fail to provide transi-

# Holistic Scale: Six Points (continued)

tions between ideas. The paper may also demonstrate little awareness of audience. Some support is included, but elaboration is not consistent or substantial. The writer's choice of words is generally adequate, but may be predictable or imprecise. The writer may also vary his or her sentence structure very little, or not at all. Usually, however, the writer has a command of the basic conventions of writing. Letter format and paragraphing may be missing.

**Score Point 2** | **A score "2" paper has the following characteristics.**
The paper is generally responsive to the prompt but includes irrelevant or loosely related material. Many "2" papers will not offer a clear opinion about the book nor cite criteria for judgment. The paper may show few signs of an overall organizational strategy and few clear transitions between ideas. Some papers may have an initial sense of purpose but then veer off-track. Support is generally unelaborated, consisting of lists or simple summary. The writer's choice of words is often imprecise or inappropriate and sentence structure is not adequately varied. The writer may show limited knowledge of the basic conventions of writing. No attempt at letter format is made.

**Score Point 1** | **A score "1" paper has the following characteristics.**
The paper may address the prompt in only a minimal or tangential way. In addition, the paper may be highly fragmentary, often a listing of ideas with little development of support. Frequently, no organizational pattern is apparent. If any attempt to support or organize ideas is exhibited, a "1" paper is too short or skeletal to achieve a higher score. There is often no sense of audience. Inappropriate word choice and errors in sentence structure may also completely hinder the paper's readability. The writer may make blatant errors in grammar, mechanics, and usage. The writer does not use a letter format or paragraphing.

**Unscorable** | **The paper is unscorable because**
- the response is not relevant to the prompt.
- the response is only a rewording of the prompt.
- the response contains an insufficient amount of writing to determine if it addresses the prompt.
- the response is a copy of a previously published work.
- the response is illegible, incomprehensible, or blank.

# Holistic Scale: Four Points

### Score Point 4

**Responses that are organized, elaborated, and highly readable attempts to clarify, explain, or present information about the specified topic. Although a score "4" paper may exhibit a few inconsistencies, such inconsistencies are eclipsed by the overall quality, coherence, and thoughtfulness of the response.**

- *The most characteristic trait of these responses is the ample and relevant support they contain; all ideas are specific and well elaborated. Such responses are also characterized by most of the following:*

  - ✓ *A unified organizational plan.* The responses have a clear organization and seem complete; if the writer employs more than one organizational strategy, all ideas still follow a logical progression. Minor inconsistencies may occur, but they do not detract from the overall order of the paper. In cases in which writers have run out of space, especially well-organized papers may still receive a "4."

  - ✓ *A marked command of written language.* These responses are fluent and clear; although some writers may not use all of the appropriate conventions of language, these responses are nevertheless quite skillfully written.

  - ✓ *Varied syntactic construction.* These responses contain compound and complex sentences.

  - ✓ *Concrete, vivid details.* All descriptions and explanations are communicated through thoughtful and effective word choices and expressions.

  - ✓ *Attention to all parts of the prompt.*

### Score Point 3

**Responses that are good efforts to clarify, explain, or present information about the specified topic. For the most part, a reader finds the paper clear, coherent, and reasonably elaborated.**

- *The following types of responses fall into the "3" category:*

  - ✓ *Papers that offer a great number of ideas, one of which is moderately elaborated, several of which are somewhat elaborated, or most of which are extended.*

  - ✓ *Papers that offer two moderately elaborated ideas.*

  - ✓ *Papers that offer one fully elaborated idea.*

- *These papers have the following characteristics:*

  - ✓ *A reasonably consistent organizational plan.* Occasional inconsistencies may be evident. Responses may also include extraneous or loosely related material.

  - ✓ *Control of written language.* Some errors in spelling, capitalization, punctuation, and/or usage may appear, but they do not unduly distract the reader.

  - ✓ *A clear understanding of the topic, although all parts of the prompt may not be addressed.*

### Score Point 2

**Responses that are only marginally successful in clarifying, explaining, or providing information about the specified topic.**

- *The following types of responses fall into the "2" category:*

  - ✓ *Papers that present a long list of unelaborated ideas.*

  - ✓ *Papers that present many ideas, most of which are extended.*

  - ✓ *Papers that present just a few ideas, at least one of which is somewhat elaborated.*

# Holistic Scale: Four Points *(continued)*

✓ *Papers that only summarize ideas; these papers exhibit no real elaboration.*

■ *The following descriptions characterize a "2" response:*

✓ *A great volume of writing that is not informative in purpose.*

✓ *An organizational plan that does not demonstrate a logical progression of thought; such a response may also exhibit obvious repetition of ideas.* Usually, these inconsistencies do not impede the reader's understanding.

✓ *Marginal control of written language.* Such responses exhibit awkward or simplistic sentence structures and limited word choices. Some errors in spelling, capitalization, punctuation, and/or usage may appear, although these errors do not impede the reader's understanding.

✓ *A limited understanding of the topic or informative task specified in the prompt.*

### Score Point 1

Responses that are unsuccessful efforts to clarify, explain, or present information about the specified topic.

■ *The following types of responses fall into the "1" category:*

✓ *Papers in which the writer has employed the wrong mode or misunderstood his or her purpose in writing.* Some of these responses may be persuasive rather than informative. In other responses, the writer does not make any effort to address the specified audience.

✓ *Papers in which the writer attempts to provide expository writing, but does so unsuccessfully.* These responses may appear as any of the following forms:

—*A brief phrase that is related to the prompt.*

—*An overly general response.* Such responses may present one or more ideas, sometimes slightly extended or elaborated, yet they do not address the prompt in any specific or meaningful way. These responses may often appear in the form of a summary or list.

—*A paper that initially focuses on the task but then drifts from the specified topic or from the specified purpose or mode.*

✓ *Papers that lack clarity.* Incomplete or illogical thoughts impede the reader's understanding. In addition, ideas are not connected in explicit or even implicit ways.

✓ *Papers in which the writer demonstrates no control of written language.* The reader's comprehension of the paper is seriously impeded by persistent errors in spelling, capitalization, punctuation, and usage.

✓ *Papers that demonstrate no organization or logic.* Information may appear in a random or repetitive way.

✓ *Papers that show little or no understanding of the topic or informative task specified in the prompt.*

# Holistic Scale: Four Points

## Score Point 4

Responses that are organized, elaborated, and highly readable attempts to address the persuasive task. Although a "4" paper may exhibit a few inconsistencies, such inconsistencies are eclipsed by the overall quality, coherence, and thoughtfulness of the response.

- *These responses offer a clear position and offer ample and convincing support for that position; all reasons and evidence are relevant and well-elaborated. Such responses are also characterized by most of the following:*

  ✓ *A unified organizational plan.* These responses have a clear organization and seem complete; if the writer employs more than one organizational strategy, all ideas still follow a logical progression. Minor inconsistencies may occur, but they do not detract from the overall order of the paper. Especially well-organized papers that end abruptly may still receive a "4."

  ✓ *A marked command of written language.* These responses are fluent and clear; although some writers may not use all of the appropriate conventions of language, these responses are nevertheless quite skillfully written.

  ✓ *Particularly thoughtful or original reasons.* Such reasons may offer an uncommon, philosophical, or wide-ranging perspective on the situation.

  ✓ *Vivid, relevant details.* All descriptions and arguments are communicated through precise, effective word choices and expressions.

  ✓ *An unusual persuasive strategy—one that departs from the usual or shows a spark of creative thinking.*

  ✓ *Attention to all parts of the prompt.*

## Score Point 3

Responses that are good efforts in addressing the persuasive task. For the most part, a reader finds the paper clear, coherent, and reasonably elaborated.

- *The following types of responses fall into the "3" category:*

  ✓ *Papers that offer great number of reasons in support of the writer's position: one may be moderately elaborated, several may be somewhat elaborated, or most may be extended.*

  ✓ *Papers that offer many supporting reasons, most of which are somewhat elaborated.*

  ✓ *Papers that offer two or more moderately elaborated supporting reasons.*

  ✓ *Responses that present only one fully elaborated reason for the writer's position; this reason must be thoroughly explained and convincing.*

- *These papers have the following characteristics:*

  ✓ *A reasonably consistent organizational plan.* Responses may include extraneous or loosely related material.

  ✓ *Control of written language.* Some minor errors in spelling, punctuation, and/or usage may appear.

  ✓ *A clear understanding of the persuasive task, although all parts of the prompt may not be addressed.*

# Holistic Scale: Four Points (continued)

## Score Point 2

**Responses that are only marginally successful attempts to address the persuasive task.**

- *The following types of responses fall into the "2" category:*

  ✓ *Papers that present a long list of unelaborated reasons.*

  ✓ *Papers that present a number of reasons, most of which are extended.*

  ✓ *Papers that present one moderately elaborated reason.*

- *The following descriptions characterize a "2" response:*

  ✓ *Writing that is not persuasive in purpose.*

  ✓ *An organizational plan that does not demonstrate a logical progression of thought; such a response may also exhibit obvious repetition of ideas.* Usually, these inconsistencies do not impede the reader's understanding.

  ✓ *Marginal control of written language.* Such responses exhibit awkward or simplistic sentence structures and limited word choices. Some errors in spelling, capitalization, punctuation, and/or usage may appear, although these errors do not impede the reader's understanding.

  ✓ *A limited understanding of the prompt.*

## Score Point 1

**Responses that are unsuccessful attempts to address the persuasive task.**

- *The following types of responses fall into the "1" category:*

  ✓ *Papers in which the writer has employed the wrong mode or misunderstood his or her purpose in writing.* Some of these responses may be expository or narrative rather than persuasive. In other responses, the writer gives information that does not support his or her position.

  ✓ *Papers in which the writer attempts to provide persuasive writing, but does so unsuccessfully.* These responses may appear as any of the following forms:

    —*A brief phrase that is related to the prompt.*

    —*An overly general response.* Such responses may present a position and one or more slightly extended reasons, yet the paper does not provide a logical or meaningful case in support of the position. Such responses may appear as summaries or lists.

    —*Responses that attend to the task but then drift from the specified topic or from the persuasive purpose.*

  ✓ *Papers that lack clarity.* Incomplete or illogical thoughts impede the reader's understanding. In addition, ideas are not connected in explicit or even implicit ways.

  ✓ *Papers in which the writer demonstrates no control of written language.* The reader's comprehension of the paper is seriously impeded by persistent errors in spelling, capitalization, punctuation, and usage.

  ✓ *Papers that demonstrate no organization or logic.* Information may appear in a random or repetitive way.

  ✓ *Papers that show no understanding of the prompt.*

# Holistic Scale: Four Points

### Score Point 4

Responses that are organized, elaborated, and highly readable attempts to present and explain an evaluation of a book. Although a "4" paper may exhibit a few inconsistencies, such inconsistencies are eclipsed by the overall quality, coherence, and thoughtfulness of the response.

- *These responses offer a clear recommendation and offer ample and convincing support for that recommendation; all reasons and evidence are relevant and well elaborated. Such responses are also characterized by most of the following:*

  ✓ *A unified organizational plan.* These responses have a clear organization and seem complete.

  ✓ *A marked command of written language.* These responses are fluent and clear; although some writers may not use all of the appropriate conventions of language, these responses are nevertheless quite skillfully written.

  ✓ *Particularly thoughtful or original reasons or criteria.* Such criteria may be uncommon or exceptionally insightful rather than general or obvious. The reasons may also show a command of literary concepts and elements.

  ✓ *Vivid, relevant details.* All descriptions and assessments are communicated through precise, effective word choices.

  ✓ *An unusual writing strategy—one that departs from the usual or shows a spark of creative thinking.*

  ✓ *Use of correct letter format and a clear conception of a specific audience.*

  ✓ *Attention to all parts of the prompt.*

### Score Point 3

Responses that are good efforts in addressing the hybrid task of explaining an opinion about a book and making a recommendation. For the most part, a reader finds the paper clear, coherent, and reasonably elaborated.

- *The following types of responses fall into the "3" category:*

  ✓ *Papers that offer many reasons in support of the writer's evaluation; one may be moderately elaborated, several may be somewhat elaborated, or most may be extended.*

  ✓ *Papers that offer at least two moderately elaborated supporting reasons.*

  ✓ *Responses that present only one fully elaborated reason.*

- *These papers have the following characteristics:*

  ✓ *A reasonably consistent organizational plan.* Responses may include some extraneous or loosely related material.

  ✓ *Control of written language.* Some errors in spelling, capitalization, punctuation, and/or usage may appear, but they do not unduly distract the reader.

  ✓ *An attempt at letter format, though it may not be entirely correct, and a conception of audience, though it may be inconsistent at times.*

  ✓ *A moderate understanding of literary elements and an ability to discuss them with reasonable skill.*

### Score Point 2

Responses that are only marginally successful attempts to recommend a course of action and explain the reasons for the recommendation.

- *The following types of responses fall into the "2" category:*

  ✓ *Papers that present a long list of unelaborated reasons.*

  ✓ *Papers that present a number of reasons, most of which are extended.*

# Holistic Scale: Four Points (continued)

✓ *Papers that present one moderately elaborated reason.*

■ *The following descriptions characterize a "2" response:*

✓ *Writing that is not persuasive or explanatory in purpose.*

✓ *An organizational plan that does not demonstrate a logical progression of thought; such a response may also exhibit obvious repetition of ideas.*

✓ *Marginal control of written language.* Such responses exhibit awkward or simplistic sentence structures and limited word choices. Some errors in spelling, capitalization, punctuation, and/or usage may appear, although these errors do not impede the reader's understanding.

✓ *No attempt at letter format beyond greeting or closing and no clear concept of audience.*

✓ *A limited understanding of literary elements.*

✓ *A limited understanding of the prompt.*

**Score Point 1**

Responses that are unsuccessful attempts to form or communicate an evaluation.

■ *The following types of responses fall into the "1" category:*

✓ *Papers in which the writer has employed the wrong mode or misunderstood his or her purpose in writing.*

✓ *Papers in which the writer attempts to provide persuasive writing, but does so unsuccessfully.* These responses may appear as any of the following forms:

—*A brief phrase that is related to the prompt.*

—*An overly general response.* Such responses may present an evaluation statement and one or more slightly extended reasons, yet the paper does not provide a logical or meaningful case in support of the evaluation. Such responses may appear as summaries or lists.

—*Responses that drift from the specified topic or from the task of recommending a course of action.*

✓ *Papers that lack clarity.* Incomplete or illogical thoughts impede the reader's understanding.

✓ *Papers in which the writer demonstrates no control of written language.* The reader's comprehension of the paper is seriously impeded by persistent errors in grammar, mechanics, and usage.

✓ *Papers that demonstrate no organization or logic.* Information may appear in a random or repetitive way.

✓ *Papers that show no attempt at letter format and no clear conception of audience.*

✓ *Papers that show no understanding of the task, including how to analyze literary elements.*

# Analytical Scale: Six Traits

## IDEAS AND CONTENT

### Score Point 5

The paper is clear, focused, and engaging. Its thoughtful, concrete details capture the reader's attention and flesh out the central theme, main idea, or story line.

- A score "5" paper has the following characteristics.

  ✓ The topic is clearly focused and manageable for a paper of its kind; it is not overly broad or scattered.
  ✓ Ideas are original and creative.
  ✓ The writer appears to be working from personal knowledge or experience.
  ✓ Key details are insightful and well considered; they are not obvious, predictable, or humdrum.
  ✓ The development of the topic is thorough and purposeful; the writer anticipates and answers the reader's questions.
  ✓ Supporting details are never superfluous or merely ornamental; every detail contributes to the whole.

### Score Point 3

The writer develops the topic in a general or basic way; although clear, the paper remains routine or broad.

- A score "3" paper has the following characteristics.

  ✓ Although the topic may be fuzzy, it is still possible to understand the writer's purpose and to predict how the paper will be developed.
  ✓ Support is present, but somewhat vague and unhelpful in illustrating the key issues or main idea; the writer makes references to his or her own experience or knowledge, but has difficulty moving from general observations to specifics.
  ✓ Ideas are understandable, yet not detailed, elaborated upon, or personalized; the writer's ideas do not reveal any deep comprehension of the topic or of the task.
  ✓ The writer does not stray from the topic, but ideas remain general or slightly implicit; more information is necessary to sketch in the gaps.

### Score Point 1

The paper does not exhibit any clear purpose or main idea. The reader must use the scattered details to infer a coherent and meaningful message.

- A score "1" paper has the following characteristics.

  ✓ The writer seems not to have truly settled on a topic; the essay reads like a series of brainstorming notes or disconnected, random thoughts.
  ✓ The thesis is a vague statement of the topic rather than a main idea about the topic; in addition, there is little or no support or detail.
  ✓ Information is very limited or vague; readers must make inferences to fill in gaps of logic or to identify any progression of ideas.
  ✓ Text may be rambling and repetitious; alternatively, the length may not be adequate for a thoughtful development of ideas.
  ✓ There is no subordination of ideas; every idea seems equally weighted, or ideas are not tied to a main idea.

# Analytical Scale: Six Traits (continued)

## ORGANIZATION

### Score Point 5

Organization enables the clear communication of the central idea or storyline. The order of information draws the reader effortlessly through the text.

- **A score "5" paper has the following characteristics.**

  ✓ The sequencing is logical and effective.
  ✓ The essay contains an interesting or inviting introduction and a satisfying conclusion.
  ✓ The pacing is carefully controlled; the writer slows down to provide explanation or elaboration when appropriate and increases the pace when necessary.
  ✓ Transitions carefully connect ideas and cue the reader to specific relationships between ideas.
  ✓ The choice of organizational structure is appropriate to the writer's purpose and audience.
  ✓ If present, the title sums up the central idea of the paper in a fresh or thoughtful way.

### Score Point 3

Organization is reasonably strong; it enables the reader to continually move forward without undue confusion.

- **A score "3" paper has the following characteristics.**

  ✓ The essay has an introduction and conclusion. However, the introduction may not be inviting or engaging; the conclusion may not knit all the paper's ideas together.
  ✓ Sequencing is logical, but predictable. Sometimes, the sequence may be so formulaic that it distracts from the content.
  ✓ At times, the sequence may not consistently support the essay's ideas; the reader may wish to mentally reorder sections or to supply transitions as he or she reads.
  ✓ Pacing is reasonably well done, although sometimes the writer moves ahead too quickly or spends too much time on unimportant details.
  ✓ At times, transitions may be fuzzy, showing unclear connections between ideas.
  ✓ If present, the title may be dull or a simple restatement of the topic or prompt.

### Score Point 1

Writing does not exhibit a sense of purpose or writing strategy. Ideas, details, or events appear to be cobbled together without any internal structure.

- **A score "1" paper has the following characteristics.**

  ✓ Sequencing needs work; one idea or event does not logically follow another. Organizational problems make it difficult for the reader to understand the main idea.
  ✓ There is no real introduction to guide the reader into the paper; neither is there any real conclusion or attempt to tie things up at the end.
  ✓ Pacing is halting or inconsistent; the writer may slow the pace or speed up at inappropriate times.
  ✓ Ideas are connected with confusing transitions; alternatively, connections are altogether absent.
  ✓ If present, the title does not accurately reflect the content of the essay.

# Analytical Scale: Six Traits (continued)

## VOICE

**Score Point 5**

The writing is expressive and engaging. In addition, the writer seems to have a clear awareness of audience and purpose.

- A score "5" paper has the following characteristics.

  ✓ The tone of the writing is appropriate for the purpose and audience of the paper.
  ✓ The reader is aware of a real person behind the text; if appropriate, the writer takes risks in revealing a personal dimension throughout the piece.
  ✓ If expository or persuasive, the writer shows a strong connection to the topic and explains why the reader should care about the issue.
  ✓ If narrative writing, the point of view is sincere, interesting, and compelling.

**Score Point 3**

The writer is reasonably genuine, but does not reveal any excitement or connection with the issue. The resulting paper is pleasant, but not truly engaging.

- A score "3" paper has the following characteristics.

  ✓ The writer offers obvious generalities instead of personal insights.
  ✓ The writer uses neutral language and a slightly flattened tone.
  ✓ The writer communicates in an earnest and pleasing manner, yet takes no risks. In only rare instances is the reader captivated or moved.
  ✓ Expository or persuasive writing does not reveal a consistent engagement with the topic; there is no attempt to build credibility with the audience.
  ✓ Narrative writing doesn't reveal a fresh or individual perspective.

**Score Point 1**

Writing is mechanical or wooden. The writer appears indifferent to the topic and/or the audience.

- A score "1" paper has the following characteristics.

  ✓ The writer shows no concern with the audience; the voice may be jarringly inappropriate for the intended reader.
  ✓ The development of the topic is so limited that no identifiable point of view is present; or the writing is so short that it offers little but a general introduction of the topic.
  ✓ The writer seems to speak in a monotone, using a voice that suppresses all excitement about the message.
  ✓ Although the writing may communicate on a functional level, the writing is ordinary and takes no risks; depending on the topic, it may be overly technical or jargonistic.

# Analytical Scale: Six Traits *(continued)*

## WORD CHOICE

**Score Point 5**

Words are precise, engaging, and unaffected. They convey the writer's message in an interesting and effective way.

- A score "5" paper has the following characteristics.

  ✓ All words are specific and appropriate. In all instances, the writer has taken care to choose the right words or phrases.
  ✓ The paper's language is natural, not overwrought; it never shows a lack of control. Clichés and jargon are rarely used.
  ✓ The paper contains energetic verbs; precise nouns and modifiers provide clarity.
  ✓ The writer uses vivid words and phrases, including sensory details; such language creates distinct images in the reader's mind.

**Score Point 3**

Despite its lack of flair, the paper's language gets the message across. It is functional and clear.

- A score "3" paper has the following characteristics.

  ✓ Words are correct and generally adequate, but lack originality or precision.
  ✓ Familiar words and phrases do not pique the reader's interest or imagination. Lively verbs and phrases perk things up occasionally, but the paper does not consistently sparkle.
  ✓ There are attempts at engaging or academic language but they sometimes seem overly showy or pretentious.
  ✓ The writing contains passive verbs, basic nouns and adjectives, and the lack of precise adverbs.

**Score Point 1**

The writer's limited vocabulary impedes communication; he or she seems to struggle for words to convey a clear message.

- A score "1" paper has the following characteristics.

  ✓ Vague language communicates an imprecise or incomplete message. The reader is left confused or unsure of the writer's purpose.
  ✓ Words are used incorrectly. In addition, frequent misuse of parts of speech impairs understanding.
  ✓ Excessive redundancy in the paper is distracting.
  ✓ The writing overuses jargon or clichés.

# Analytical Scale: Six Traits *(continued)*

## SENTENCE FLUENCY

### Score Point 5

Sentences are thoughtfully constructed and sentence structure is varied throughout the paper. When read aloud, the writing is fluent and rhythmic.

- **A score "5" paper has the following characteristics.**

  ✓ The sentences are constructed so that meaning is clear to the reader.

  ✓ Sentences vary in length and in structure.

  ✓ Varied sentence beginnings add interest and clarity.

  ✓ The writing has a steady beat; the reader is able to read the text effortlessly, without confusion or stumbling.

  ✓ Dialogue, if used, is natural. Any fragments are used purposefully and contribute to the paper's style.

  ✓ Thoughtful connectives and transitions between sentences reveal how the paper's ideas work together.

### Score Point 3

The text maintains a steady rhythm, but the reader may find it more flat or mechanical than fluent or musical.

- **A score "3" paper has the following characteristics.**

  ✓ Sentences are usually grammatical and unified, but they are routine rather than artful. The writer has not paid a great deal of attention to how the sentences sound.

  ✓ There is some variation in sentence length and structure as well as in sentence beginnings. Not all sentences are constructed exactly the same way.

  ✓ The reader may have to search for transitional words and phrases that show how sentences relate to one another. Sometimes, such context clues are entirely absent when they should be present.

  ✓ Although sections of the paper invite expressive oral reading, the reader may also encounter many wooden or awkward sections.

### Score Point 1

The reader will encounter challenges in reading the choppy or confusing text; meaning may be significantly obscured by the errors in sentence construction.

- **A score "1" paper has the following characteristics.**

  ✓ The sentences do not "hang together." They are run-on, incomplete, monotonous, or awkward.

  ✓ Phrasing often sounds too sing-song, not natural. The paper does not invite expressive oral reading.

  ✓ Nearly all the sentences begin the same way and they may all follow the same pattern (e.g. subject-verb-object). The result may be a monotonous repetition of sounds.

  ✓ Endless connectives or a complete lack of connectives create a confused muddle of language.

# Analytical Scale: Six Traits *(continued)*

## CONVENTIONS

### Score Point 5

**Standard writing conventions (e.g. spelling, punctuation, capitalization, grammar, usage, and paragraphing) are used correctly and in a way that aids the reader's understanding. Any errors tend to be minor; the piece is nearly ready for publication.**

■ **A score "5" paper has the following characteristics.**

✓ Paragraphing is regular and enhances the organization of the paper.

✓ Grammar and usage are correct and add clarity to the text as a whole. Sometimes, the writer may manipulate conventions in a controlled way—especially grammar and spelling—for stylistic effect.

✓ Punctuation is accurate; it enables the reader to move through the text with understanding and ease.

✓ The writer's understanding of capitalization skills is evident throughout the paper.

✓ Most words, even difficult ones, are spelled correctly.

✓ The writing is long and complex enough to show the writer using a wide range of conventions skillfully.

### Score Point 3

**The writer exhibits an awareness of a limited set of standard writing conventions and uses them to enhance the paper's readability. Although the writer shows control, at times errors distract the reader or impede communication. Moderate editing is required for publication.**

■ **A score "3" paper has the following characteristics.**

✓ Paragraphs are used, but may begin in the wrong places or run together sections that should be separate paragraphs.

✓ Conventions may not be correct all of the time. However, problems with grammar and usage are usually not serious enough to distort meaning.

✓ Terminal (end-of-sentence) punctuation is usually correct; internal punctuation (e.g. commas, apostrophes, semicolons, parentheses) may be missing or wrong.

✓ On common words, spelling is usually correct or phonetic.

✓ Most words are capitalized correctly, but the writer's command of more sophisticated capitalization skills is inconsistent.

### Score Point 1

**There are errors in spelling, punctuation, usage and grammar, capitalization, and/or paragraphing that seriously impede the reader's comprehension. Extensive editing is required for publication.**

■ **A score "1" paper has the following characteristics.**

✓ Paragraphing is missing, uneven, or too frequent. Most of the paragraphs do not reinforce or support the organizational structure of the paper.

✓ Errors in grammar/usage are very common and distracting; such errors also affect the paper's meaning.

✓ Punctuation, including terminal punctuation, is often missing or incorrect.

✓ Even on common words, spelling errors are frequent.

✓ Capitalization is haphazard or reveals the writer's understanding of only the simplest rules.

✓ The paper must be read once just to decode the language and then again to capture the paper's meaning.

# Sample A: Expository Writing

**PROMPT**

Think about what kind of music you like best. Write a well-organized paper stating your preference and explaining why you prefer that kind of music over others.

Did you know that music can soothe even the most savage beast? Not that I'm saying I am a savage beast. Let me explain . . .

I have listened to many different kinds of music over the years. These have included pop, classic rock, alternative, and hard rock. I have enjoyed these types of music for different reasons. Who can't sing along to a good harmonizing pop song? Who would argue that classic rock music has wonderful guitar players? Who doesn't find the musical sounds of alternative bands hard to resist? I think all music is great. But if I have to choose the one I like the most, I would say it's hard rock music.

After a hard day at school, I listen to hard rock music to relax. Believe it or not, the banging drums and the smashing sounds of guitars help reenergize me. I can't help it. When I crank up the music, I find myself playing an air guitar or banging away on my dresser with pencils. The booming bass draws me in like a moth to a light and chips away all my worries. I become a "rock star," and nothing else seems to matter. As an added bonus, the blaring music and my jumping all around also annoys my sister immensely.

Since I am now in 7th grade, the challenges at school have gotten harder for me. In middle school, you have more than one teacher, so you can easily get 6 homework assignments in one day. That can be tough especially when you have other activities that you are responsible for. Like me for instance, last Tuesday I had to study for two tests and stay after school until 6 pm for band practice. Another challenge in middle

# Sample A: Expository Writing *(continued)*

school is that kids can be mean. Everyday I see kids picking on other kids just because they are different. For example, a girl in my art class has a certain band's sticker on her notebook. These other girls started to make fun of her because they like a different kind of music. But you know what, music can help in these situations—even hard rock music. The lyrics let me know that everyone has challenging times, and inside we're all the same. Therefore, we should try to treat people who are different with respect even if we don't agree with them.

You can see that hard rock music does help me relax and learn something about the world. So the next time you feel tired or bothered just follow my advice: Go home, get a glass of soda, pull up your favorite easy chair, and listen to some soothing hard rock music. Because after all, music does soothe even the most savage beast!

# Sample A Evaluation: Expository Writing

**Six Point Holistic Scale**

**Rating: 6 points**

**Comments:** The paper is focused and shows a clear understanding of the writing situation. Organization is consistent and unified, although the writer seems at risk of veering off-topic in the fourth paragraph. Ideas are clear and well elaborated with anecdotes, vivid details, and figurative language. The rhetorical questions in the first two paragraphs and the recommendation in the last paragraph show a clear awareness of audience and a fresh, natural voice. The writer also shows control of the written language. Sentences are varied, and few errors are made in grammar, mechanics, and usage.

**Four Point Holistic Scale**

**Rating: 4 points**

**Comments:** The writer presents relevant and well-elaborated reasons to support his preference of hard rock music. The paper has a clear sense of order, and, although one anticipates a digression in the fourth paragraph, ideas do progress logically throughout. The writer possesses a control of the written language, making few grammar, usage, mechanics mistakes. The paper contains a variety of concrete and vivid details, many drawn from the writer's own experience. Sentence structure is varied; in the third paragraph, for example, the writer includes simple, compound, and complex sentences. The writer also uses vivid and clever words and expressions, such as "music soothes the savage beast," "booming bass," and "like a moth to light."

**Six Trait Analytic Scale**

**Ratings**

| | |
|---|---|
| **Ideas and Content: 5** | **Word Choice: 5** |
| **Organization: 4** | **Sentence Fluency: 5** |
| **Voice: 5** | **Conventions: 5** |

**Comments:** The paper includes relevant anecdotes and details that fully develop the topic and engage the reader. The organization is logical, and the pacing is well controlled. The writer's voice is unique and genuine, especially when he comments on the challenges middle school students encounter. Word choices are precise yet not overdone, making the language natural and appealing. Sentence variety creates an easy flow when the essay is read aloud. The writer demonstrates a good grasp of standard writing conventions. Errors in usage and mechanics are minor.

# Sample B: Expository Writing

PROMPT

Think about what kind of music you like best. Write a well-organized paper stating your preference and explaining why you prefer that kind of music over others.

---

Music helps children learn about culture. It also soothes people.

I have listened to many different kinds of music. Classical music doesn't do the trick for me anymore. When I want to relax I listen to hard rock music. I like the banging drums and the guitar sound. It helps me get over a hard day at school. It also annoys my sister.

I am now in 7th grade, school is harder for me. The lyrics let me know that alot of people go through hard times but its ok.

Hard rock music is my favorite because there are alot of radio stations that play it in my town. My alarm clock is tuned to a hard rock station. I wake up to hard rock music. Sometimes my Dad lets me listen to it in his car.

The next time you want to relax listen to some soothing hard rock music. Because hard rock music is the greatest!

# Sample B Evaluation: Expository Writing

**Six Point Holistic Scale**

**Rating: 3 points**

**Comments:** The writer clearly focuses on the topic and provides reasons for preferring hard rock music. The apparent thesis in the first paragraph, however, is weakly supported. For example, the second paragraph does not provide readers with any idea of how music can teach children about culture; it focuses instead on music as soothing. The paper is organized but lacks a sense of completeness. Elaboration is present but is not sufficient to fully explain the writer's ideas; at times, the essay reads like a list. Although there is an awareness of audience, the writer shows little variation in sentence structure, and word choice is limited. Mechanics and spelling mistakes are evident, but they are not distracting.

**Four Point Holistic Scale**

**Rating: 2 points**

**Comments:** The paper clearly shows that the writer prefers hard rock music, but the majority of reasons are only extended. An organizational strategy is apparent, but is flawed by a lack of unity. For example, the topic sentence in the first paragraph does not list all the reasons discussed in the body paragraphs. Sentence structure is repetitive and simple, and word choice is limited. The writer does make mistakes in spelling, capitalization, and punctuation.

**Six Trait Analytic Scale**

**Ratings**

| | |
|---|---|
| **Ideas and Content: 2** | **Word Choice: 2** |
| **Organization: 3** | **Sentence Fluency: 2** |
| **Voice: 2** | **Conventions: 2** |

**Comments:** The writer attempts to define the topic, but information is very limited. The paper's organization moves the reader through the text without confusion; however, ideas are strung together without direct connections. The writer's voice is mechanical, revealing very little about the person. The use of the exclamation point in the last sentence does communicate some enthusiasm, but the rest of the paper has not shown a fresh or engaging tone. Language is functional, but the text is choppy due to a lack of sentence variety. Errors in spelling, punctuation, and capitalization are noticeable but do not hinder readability.

# Sample C: Expository Writing

**PROMPT**

Think about what kind of music you like best. Write a well-organized paper stating your preference and explaining why you prefer that kind of music over others.

I used to listen to classic music. Pop music is ok to. And altrnetive music is good. I like all kinds of music but hard rock music is my favrite. It's cool and you should listen to it to. I listen to hard rock music when I get home from school and want to relax. I listen to it in the car and when I wake up. My sister hates my music but I don't care I listen to it anyways. She tells me to turn it down but I don't. Some kids at my school like hard rock music. Some kids don't. School is hard. Everyone should listen to whatever music they like and not make fun of other people. I don't like country music alot but some of my friends do and that's ok they can listen to it. I have alot of cds. You can get hard rock cds at most any record stores. They have all different bands. You can even by stickers to put on your notebook and tshirts to. The radio plays hard rock music to. There's this one staten that I listen to that plays it all the time. I like hard rock music and you should to. Hard rock music is the greatest!

# Sample C Evaluation: Expository Writing

| | |
|---|---|
| **Six Point Holistic Scale** | **Rating: 1 point**<br>**Comments:** The writer addresses the topic by providing a main idea statement; however, the ideas presented in the writing do not support an informative purpose. Instead, much of the paper is narrative. Support is vague and does not sufficiently explain why the writer prefers hard rock music. The paper lacks organization; the writer's thoughts are loosely connected and no paragraphing is attempted, a sign that the writer is jotting ideas in a random way. The writer makes many errors in spelling, punctuation, and usage. There is no consistent sense of audience, word choice is limited, and sentence structure is repetitive and simple. |
| **Four Point Holistic Scale** | **Rating: 1 point**<br>**Comments:** The writer makes an unsuccessful attempt at informative writing. The paper addresses the topic; however, the ideas do not sufficiently explain why the writer prefers hard rock music. Instead, the writer simply lists thoughts about hard rock music that are not clearly connected, causing the reader some confusion. Errors in spelling, usage, and mechanics are evident, and organization is random. |
| **Six Trait Analytic Scale** | **Ratings** |

**Ideas and Content: 1**       **Word Choice: 2**

**Organization: 1**       **Sentence Fluency: 1**

**Voice: 2**       **Conventions: 1**

**Comments:** The paper does not have a clear sense of purpose or direction. Details read like random thoughts, and connections between the ideas are confusing. The writer's voice is sincere, but the writer's choice of words do not help convey a strong message. Sentence structure is simple, creating a choppy flow when read aloud. Paragraphing is missing, punctuation is incorrect, and spelling errors are obvious. Extensive editing would be required for publication.

# Sample A: Persuasive Writing

Imagine that a local builder found an ancient campsite while clearing land to build a badly needed school. Should the builder be allowed to proceed, or should building stop while archaeologists study the site? Local schools are overcrowded, and archaeologists estimate it could take as long as a year to complete their study. Write a letter to the editor of a local paper stating your position and supporting it with convincing reasons.

Dear Editor:

I know it is important to make discoveries at the ancient campsite, but I think a year is too long to wait to start building a new school. I think we should give the archaeologists a shorter time to dig so we don't spend another whole school year crowded into an old school building. My reasons are that technology can help both projects get done faster and that people on both sides want the best for history and for children.

Technology can help in two ways. I think the archaeologists should get one of those scanners that lets them look underground. If they see anything out of the ordinary, they should start digging immediately. If they find nothing in a period of 5 months, we should start to build the foundation for our new school. During the time when the archaeologists are looking at the site, the new school can be designed and we can use computer programs to plan all of the materials that will be needed and figure out the most efficient way to do the job. That way, as soon as the archaeologists finish, we can be ready to start work right away and finish the school faster.

If I was an archaeologist, of course I would want to dig up whatever is down there. They might learn more about early humans or maybe even find something that can confirm the way the dinosaurs died, and then they would want to keep digging. But even if I was an archaeologist, I would probably still want the best for the children. After all, archaeologists probably have kids, too. The archaeologists should try to finish their project as soon as they can so that the school will be ready by the next school

# Sample A: Persuasive Writing *(continued)*

year. If I was an archaeologist I would not want my work to force kids to stay crowded in their old school.

If I was an administrator, obviously I would want to build the school, but I would probably be interested in finding out what was at the site. If there were fossils or artifacts to be found I would have the archaeologists start digging. Their discoveries might give us further things to study in our new school, and our school would be recognized as the place where an important discovery was made. Finding fossils at our new school will give us an advantage, but stopping construction for a whole year would mean the old school will still be crowded and will need extra teachers to provide supervision for the students.

The best solution to this problem is to limit the delay caused by digging at the site. The archaeologists and builders should use technology to speed up the process so construction of the new school can begin in time for the school to be ready for the next school year. We deserve to go to a new school that is not overcrowded.

# Sample A Evaluation: Persuasive Writing

| | |
|---|---|
| **Six Point Holistic Scale** | **Rating: 5 points**<br>**Comments:** The writer clearly addresses the prompt and proposes a compromise position. In fact, the writer shows insight into the situation by considering the two positions on opposite sides of the issue and finding common ground between them. Support is detailed and thoughtful, showing the writer's obvious engagement with the issue. Organization is logical, and sentence structure is varied. The writer demonstrates a command of the conventions of written language, with few if any errors in spelling, punctuation, grammar, and usage. |
| **Four Point Holistic Scale** | **Rating: 4 points**<br>**Comments:** The writer provides two moderately elaborated reasons for the stated position. In the first, the writer demonstrates a broad view of the situation, and in the second reason he considers multiple perspectives, focusing on the interests in history and children that both sides share. Ideas are thoughtful, wide-ranging, and organized clearly. The writer demonstrates control of written language, with few if any errors in spelling, capitalization, punctuation, and usage. Although the writing might have been a bit more concise, sentences are clear and fluent. |
| **Six Trait Analytic Scale** | **Ratings** |

**Ratings**

| | |
|---|---|
| **Ideas and Content: 4** | **Word Choice: 3** |
| **Organization: 4** | **Sentence Fluency: 5** |
| **Voice: 4** | **Conventions: 5** |

**Comments:** The writer identifies a clear position and considers multiple perspectives, although the ideas sometimes lack specificity. Organization fits the writer's purpose and ideas progress logically. The writer demonstrates a keen involvement with the topic, but uses a fair and calm voice as he discusses possible concerns from opposing viewpoints. Word choice is correct and adequate to communicate the writer's ideas. Sentences vary in length and structure and clearly communicate the writer's message. The writer demonstrates control over the conventions of written language; paragraphing, grammar, usage, punctuation, capitalization, and spelling are generally correct.

# Sample B: Persuasive Writing

**PROMPT**

Imagine that a local builder found an ancient campsite while clearing land to build a badly needed school. Should the builder be allowed to proceed, or should building stop while archaeologists study the site? Local schools are overcrowded, and archaeologists estimate it could take as long as a year to complete their study. Write a letter to the editor of a local paper stating your position and supporting it with convincing reasons.

If my school was in this position, I would say that we can't wait a whole year to start building a new school. I would tell the archaeologists to get one of those scanners that lets them look underground. If they find nothing in a period of 5 months, I would tell them you have till the end of the day to get all of your equipment off this property. Then the administrator's office should bring loads of dirt to fill in what the archaeologists dug up. After waiting about a week for the dirt to settle in the ground, they could start to build the formation for the school.

If I was a archaeologist, of course I would want to dig whatever is down there. They might find something that can confirm the way the dinousours died, and then they would want to keep digging. But even if I was a archaeologist, I would probably still want the best for the children. The archaeologist should try to finish their project as soon as they can so that the school will be ready by the next school year.

If I was a administrator, I would want to build the school, but I would probably be interested in finding out what was at the site. Any discoveries might give us further things to study in our new school. Finding fossils at our new school will give us an advantage, but stopping construction for a whole year would mean the old school will still be crowded and will need extra teachers to provide supervision for the students. In a way I understand both sides because they both have advantages. The smart decision is to limit the delay caused by digging at the site.

# Sample B Evaluation: Persuasive Writing

**Six Point Holistic Scale**

**Rating: 3 points**

**Comments:** The writer focuses on the persuasive task and develops a thoughtful compromise position. Ideas are organized logically, but the paper lacks a sense of completeness. Reasons are somewhat supported, though support is not as persuasive, detailed, or on-topic as it might have been; much of the paper is taken up with narrative details, showing the writer's preoccupation with the process that leads to a resolution of the problem. Word choice is adequate but limited, and there is little sense of audience. The writer generally follows the conventions of written language, with only minor errors in spelling, punctuation, grammar, and usage.

**Four Point Holistic Scale**

**Rating: 2 points**

**Comments:** The writer fashions a compromise position, but his ideas are only extended rather than fully elaborated. In addition, too much of the paper is a narrative of the steps the writer recommends. Organization is logical, and sentences are generally complete. Ideas and word choice are vague and general rather than detailed and specific. Errors in spelling, capitalization, punctuation, and usage are minor and do not interfere with communication.

**Six Trait Analytic Scale**

**Ratings**

| | |
|---|---|
| **Ideas and Content: 3** | **Word Choice: 3** |
| **Organization: 3** | **Sentence Fluency: 3** |
| **Voice: 3** | **Conventions: 3** |

**Comments:** The writer addresses the topic and provides clear, but not detailed, ideas. Organization is logical, although the introduction and conclusion are weak and connections between ideas are sometimes unclear. The writer's voice, while pleasant, shows a detachment from the topic, and there is no attempt to reveal a consistent or forceful personality to the reader. Word choice is generally correct and adequate. Sentences are usually grammatical and vary in structure somewhat. Some paragraphing is missing at the paper's beginning and end, but errors in grammar, usage, and spelling do not interfere with the writer's meaning.

# Sample C: Persuasive Writing

**PROMPT**

Imagine that a local builder found an ancient campsite while clearing land to build a badly needed school. Should the builder be allowed to proceed, or should building stop while archaeologists study the site? Local schools are overcrowded, and archaeologists estimate it could take as long as a year to complete their study. Write a letter to the editor of a local paper stating your position and supporting it with convincing reasons.

If my school was in this position I would have to say to the archeologist for them to get one of those scanners and look underground. If they find nothing, I would tell them you have till the end of the day to get all of your equipment off this property. Then I would call the administrators office and tell them to bring so many loads of dirt to fill in what the archeologist dug up and then wait about a week for the dirt to settle. The dirt has to settle or the building wont be steady.

If I was a archeologist of course I would want to dig what ever is down there. I would want to hurry an get the project over with so that they could start building the new school for the kids so they wont be crowded in there old school.

If I was a administrator I would want to build the school but if there are fossils maybe we should build the school somewhere else. There is an empty shopping center not to far from our school that we could tear down. Then the archoelogists could dig.

That's what you have to think about will it bring advantages or disadvantages. Now you think which one would you want to be, a archeologist or an administrator. To be an administrator you can't approve that kids can bring knifes and guns to school. To be an archeologist you also have to make smart decisions like if it is the right place to dig to pull arterfacts up or it will be broke, things like that. That is what I think about this. By the way I am for both sides because they both have good advantages.

# Sample C Evaluation: Persuasive Writing

**Six Point Holistic Scale**

**Rating: 1 point**

**Comments:** The writer fails to take a persuasive position and support is confused and extended weakly at best. Irrelevant information is included and the paper feels incoherent or incomplete. There is an inadequate and inconsistent sense of audience, and the writer demonstrates only limited control over the conventions of written language, with awkward, fragmentary, and run-on sentences. Meaning is often difficult to make out. Errors in spelling, punctuation, grammar, and usage are numerous.

**Four Point Holistic Scale**

**Rating: 1 point**

**Comments:** The response attempts to be persuasive in nature, but the writer never chooses a position on the topic. The paper drifts into explaining narrative steps and then provides a significant digression about archaeologists and administrators rather than providing clear support for a persuasive position. The writer does attempt an organizational structure, but ideas are so poorly developed that the paper remains thoroughly confusing. The writer demonstrates a limited control over the conventions of written language, with awkward and unclear sentences, incomplete and run-on sentences, and errors in spelling, grammar, usage, and word choice.

**Six Trait Analytic Scale**

**Ratings**

| | |
|---|---|
| **Ideas and Content: 1** | **Word Choice: 1** |
| **Organization: 2** | **Sentence Fluency: 2** |
| **Voice: 1** | **Conventions: 2** |

**Comments:** The paper has no clear purpose and the writer includes limited, unclear, and irrelevant ideas. The writer's organization is somewhat logical, although the paper still feels fragmentary and incomplete. The writer seems unaware of the intended audience for the piece and uses a voice inappropriate for a letter to the editor. Word choice is limited, and occasionally words are misused. Sentences use a variety of structures but are often incomplete, run-on, or awkward. The numerous errors in grammar, usage, punctuation, and spelling are distracting.

# Sample A: Friendly Letter of Recommendation

**PROMPT**

Which of the short stories or books that you have read for school over the past two years influenced you the most? Choose a short story or book and write a friendly letter recommending it.

Dear Megan,

How are you? I'm doing fine. Anyway, I am writing to tell you about a story I just read called "Rikki-Tikki-Tavi" by Rudyard Kipling. I think you should read it because most of the characters are animals and it has a lot of exciting action. In a way, even though the characters are animals, it influenced me to be more confident about trying new challenges.

The animal characters in the story are Rikki Tikki, a very clever and curious mongoose, Darzee, a very loud annoying Tailorbird, and his smart, cunning wife. There is also Nag, the horrible King Cobra, and his wife Nagaina, who also is a King Cobra. The animals all talk to each other, which makes the story more interesting. The writer, Rudyard Kipling, does a good job of describing the actions of the animals vividly. It's like he watched mongooses and cobras moving and wrote down the most vivid descriptions he could of the way they moved. I know how much you like animals, so I'm sure you'll love that part of the story. The human characters are a boy named Teddy and his parents who adopt Rikki. They are nice, but they don't understand any of what the animals say to each other. The story takes place in the bathrooms and gardens of their bungalow in India.

Rikki comes to live with the family after a huge storm flushes him out of his burrow. Teddy finds him and takes him to his home. He lets Rikki warm up by the fire, and then feeds him. Rikki stays with the family and he sleeps with Teddy. The mother does not fancy this, but is soon convinced that the small mongoose would not harm her son.

The real action starts the next day. After breakfast Rikki goes out to explore the garden. He meets Darzee and his wife. They are very distressed because Nag ate one

# Sample A: Friendly Letter of Recommendation (cont.)

of their babies. At that moment, Nag crawls out from the bushes and tries to trick Rikki by distracting him while Nagaina tries to bite him. Rikki leaps just as Nagaina strikes underneath him. Angry that she missed, Nagaina and Nag leave.

That night Rikki waits in the bathroom for Nag. When the serpent slithers in, talking about how he will kill Teddy's father, Rikki attacks Nag by gripping him by the head. A mongoose's job is to attack and kill cobras. When Teddy's dad comes to shower, he sees that Rikki protected him from Nag and is very grateful.

The next day Rikki is sore from the thrashing of the battle, but he quickly finds out where the snakes' nest is. Darzee's wife makes a distraction so he can destroy the nest. Darzee's wife pretends her wing is broken, leading Nagaina away from the nest. Rikki cracks each cobra egg until one egg is left. While he is doing that, though, Nagaina corners Teddy. I shouldn't tell you any more because you should read it yourself. The battle between Rikki and Nagaina is exciting. You'll really get into the story and root for Rikki to win.

The cool thing about the character of Rikki Tikki Tavi is that he is a young mongoose who has never tried living with humans or fighting cobras before. He isn't sure what to do sometimes but he tries anyway and gets more confident when he succeeds. I know it's just a story but I thought he was pretty inspiring. Anyway, let me know what you think after you have read the story. I think you'll like the animal characters and the exciting action. I've got to run for now. Take care.

Your friend,

Shannon

# Sample A Evaluation: Friendly Letter of Recommendation

**Six Point Holistic Scale**

**Rating: 5 points**
**Comments:** The letter offers a clear recommendation based on thoughtful criteria; the last criterion, that the story influenced the writer to be more confident in the face of challenges, is especially reflective and sophisticated. The writer adequately supports the reasons for the recommendation, although the lengthy summary seems to support the "exciting action" criterion at the expense of the other criteria. The writer clearly shows involvement with both the topic and her reader. Organization is logical and control of written language is evident; sentences are generally complete and well constructed, word choices are specific, and the letter generally follows conventions of mechanics, usage, and spelling.

**Four Point Holistic Scale**

**Rating: 4 points**
**Comments:** The letter is unified, easy to read, and engaging. Ideas are clearly organized and well supported with thoughtful reasons and clear paraphrases of and references to the book. The letter shows insight by analyzing the main character and applying his experience to human life outside the story, particularly the writer's own experiences. The writer also uses a lively voice and precise details. Sentences are complete, and a variety of sentence lengths are used. Word choices are specific and often sophisticated. The letter generally follows conventions of mechanics, usage, and spelling. The letter also follows standard letter format.

**Six Trait Analytic Scale**

**Ratings**

| | |
|---|---|
| **Ideas and Content: 4** | **Word Choice: 5** |
| **Organization: 4** | **Sentence Fluency: 5** |
| **Voice: 5** | **Conventions: 5** |

**Comments:** The writer's ideas are clear and insightful. The writer organizes ideas logically and her voice shows involvement with the audience and the topic. Word choice is often specific and apt. Sentences are complete and use a variety of lengths and structures. The writer's use of paragraphing, grammar, usage, punctuation, and spelling conventions is sound.

# Sample B: Friendly Letter of Recommendation

**PROMPT**

Which of the short stories or books that you have read for school over the past two years influenced you the most? Choose a short story or book and write a friendly letter recommending it.

Dear Megan,

How are you? I'm doing pretty good. Jackson is being his regular terrorist self, but what can you expect from a two-year-old. How is your brother? Is he being a brat too? Any way I am writing to tell you about a story I just read called. Rikki Tickki Tavi, by Rudyard Kipling.

The characters in the story are Rikki Tikki, a very clever and curious mongoose, Darzee, a very loud annoying Tailbird, and his smart, cunning wife. There is also a cute little muskrat, Chuchundra, and Nag, the horrible King Cobra, and his wife Nagaina, who also is a King Cobra. The story all takes place through the bathrooms of a big bungalow in a Segowlee cantonment. A huge storm comes and flushes Rikki out of his burrow. A little boy named Teddy finds him and takes him to his home, where he lives with his mother and father. Teddy lets Rikki warm up by the fire, then feeds him. Rikki stays with the family and he sleeps with Teddy. The mother does not fancy this, but is soon convinced that the small mongoose would not harm her son.

The next day after breakfast Rikki goes out to explore. He meets Darzee and his wife. They are very distressed. "Our egg fell from the nest last night and Nag ate it," they told Rikki sadly. "Who is this fierce Nag?" asked the mongoose. They then told Rikki the story of Nag. Nag listened from the bushes behind Rikki. "Where can I find this devil snake?" Rikki asked. At that moment, Nag crawled out from the bushes. Rikki turned to stare at him. nag warned him to stay away, for tonight he was going to kill Teddy's father, also known as the huge man. "Watch out, behind you!" sang Darzee. Rikki leaped up into the sky, just as Nagaina struck underneath him. Angry that she had missed, Nagaina angrily slid next to Nag. As they continue talking, Rikki

# Sample B: Friendly Letter of Recommendation *(cont.)*

figures out where Nagaina's eggs were and when Nag was going to attack the huge man.

That night Rikki was waiting for Nag. When the serpent slithered in, Rikki attacked Nag by gripping him by the head. A mongoose's job is to attack and kill cobras. Soon Nag was dead. When the huge man came to shower, he saw that Rikki had protected him from Nag and was very grateful.

The next day Rikki was sore from the thrashing of last night's battle, but he quickly remembered where the snake's nest was. He ran to Darzee's wife and asked her to make a distraction so he could destroy the nest. Darzee's wife ran to where Nagaina was and pretended her wing was broken, leading Nagaina into the stables. Rikki ran to the nest and cracked each egg until one egg was left. Just then, Darzee flew down to Rikki. "Rikki come fast! Nagaina has Teddy cornered! About to strike!" she said. Rikki carried the egg to Teddy's room, and like swift lightning, got between Teddy and Nagaina. He showed her the egg and told her this was the last one that wasn't crushed. She tried to explain how she must kill the son of the huge man who killed Nag, but Rikki corrected her by telling her that he had killed Nag. In fear now, Nagaina grabbed the egg and dashed away, but not before Rikki had grabbed hold of her tail. Rikki followed her into her hole. Darzee began to sing his sad song of death, because not one mongoose had ever gone down into a Cobra's hole and returned. But Rikki . . . well, you'll just have to read the story to find out what happened to Rikki, Teddy, and the others.

Let me know what you think after you have read the story. I've got to run for now. I hope we can get together soon. Take care.

Your friend,

Shannon

# Sample B Evaluation: Friendly Letter of Recommendation

| | |
|---|---|
| **Six Point Holistic Scale** | **Rating: 3 points**<br>**Comments:** The recommendation is vague and comes only at the end of the letter. The writer primarily summarizes the book rather than giving reasons for recommending it. The summary, however, is beautifully written, smoothly integrating quotations into the writer's own sentences. Throughout the paper, the voice is lively and engaging, sentences are complete, and a variety of sentence lengths are used. Word choices are specific. The letter generally follows conventions of mechanics, usage, and grammar, although some minor errors are present. |
| **Four Point Holistic Scale** | **Rating: 2 points**<br>**Comments:** The letter does not fit the persuasive purpose of the prompt. The recommendation is vague, and the writer primarily summarizes the book rather than giving reasons for recommending it. However, the writer does demonstrate strong control of written language. Organization is logical, sentences are complete, and a variety of sentence lengths are used. Word choices are specific and frequently sophisticated. The letter generally follows conventions of mechanics, usage, and spelling. |
| **Six Trait Analytic Scale** | **Ratings**<br><br>**Ideas and Content: 2**  **Word Choice: 4**<br>**Organization: 4**  **Sentence Fluency: 4**<br>**Voice: 3**  **Conventions: 5**<br><br>**Comments:** The letter lacks a sense of purpose, and ideas included are merely a restatement of the plot of the story chosen. The writer does, however, organize ideas clearly. The writer's voice is fresh and engaging, particularly in the introduction and conclusion. Word choice is often specific and even sophisticated. Sentences are complete and use a variety of lengths. The writer's use of paragraphing, grammar, usage, punctuation, and spelling conventions is generally sound. |

# Sample C: Friendly Letter of Recommendation

> **PROMPT**
>
> Which of the short stories or books that you have read for school over the past two years influenced you the most? Choose a short story or book and write a friendly letter recommending it.

I am writing to tell about a story I just read called *Rikki Tickki Tavi*, by Rudyard Kipling. The characters in the story are Rikki Tikki, a very clever and curious mongoose, Darzee, a very loud annoying Tailbird, and his smart, cunning wife. There is also a cute little muskrat, Chuchundra, and Nag, the horrible King Cobra, and his wife Nagaina, who also is a King Cobra. Cobras have hoods around there heads and a big spot that looks like an eye on the hood. The story all takes place through the bathrooms of a big bungalow in a Segowlee cantonment. A huge storm comes and gets Rikki out of his burrow. A little boy named Teddy finds him and takes him to his home, where he lives with his mother and father. A mongoose's job is to attack and kill cobras. Rikki kills the cobras and destroys there eggs so the can't bother the humans anymore. I think my aunt Denise would like to have a liitle mongoose like Rikki for a pet because she hates snakes. Once there was a snake in her house just like Nag and Nagaina were in Teddy's house in the book. She was so scared she didnt go back for three days and the snake wasnt even poisonous like the cobras in this story. So in a way the humans are brave for even staying there but there also lucky to have Rikki. You just have to read the story to find out what happened to Rikki, Teddy, and the others.

# Sample C Evaluation: Friendly Letter of Recommendation

**Six Point Holistic Scale**

**Rating: 2 points**
**Comments:** The writing is related to the topic but contains much extraneous information and no recommendation or reasons. In addition, the letter appears to have no specific audience. Sentences are generally complete, however, and a few word choices are specific. Errors in mechanics, usage, and spelling do not interfere with the writer's message.

**Four Point Holistic Scale**

**Rating: 1 point**
**Comments:** The letter does not fit the persuasive purpose of the prompt. No recommendation or reasons are included. The letter also periodically drifts to discuss irrelevant content. No organizational pattern is apparent, and letter format is not attempted. Sentences are generally complete, however, and errors in mechanics, usage, and spelling do not interfere with communication.

**Six Trait Analytic Scale**

**Ratings**

| | |
|---|---|
| **Ideas and Content: 1** | **Word Choice: 2** |
| **Organization: 2** | **Sentence Fluency: 3** |
| **Voice: 2** | **Conventions: 2** |

**Comments:** The letter fails to exhibit a clear purpose or make a recommendation. Organization is haphazard. The writer's voice is sincere, but does not seem to be consistently addressing a reader. Only a few word choices are specific. Sentences are generally complete, but paragraphing is not attempted. Errors in grammar, usage, punctuation, and spelling are noticeable but not serious.

# Examining News

**DIRECTIONS:** Circle 1, 2, or 3 below to indicate your evaluation of each item.

| **Evaluation Scale:** | 1 = Not at all | 2 = To some extent | 3 = Successfully |
| --- | --- | --- | --- |

- The student can identify the purposes of news reports.    1   2   3

- The student can identify news values and understands the types of news stories that usually focus on each value.    1   2   3

- With a group, the student identifies news stories demonstrating each of the four news values and explains how each story demonstrates its primary value.    1   2   3

- The student can recognize differences in the presentation of the details of a news story in newspaper and television reports.    1   2   3

- The student can recognize differences in the presentation of a news story's visuals in newspaper and television reports.    1   2   3

- The student effectively researches a story reported both in the newspaper and on television.    1   2   3

- The student creates a chart that adequately identifies the differences in newspaper and television reports on the same story.    1   2   3

- The student explains which story gave him or her a better understanding of the issue and why.    1   2   3

- The student explains which story had the greater emotional impact and why.    1   2   3

- The student explains what he or she thinks was the editor or producer's purpose in running the story.    1   2   3

- The student clearly presents to the class the differences between the two reports of the chosen story.    1   2   3

- The student's presentation cites evidence from the two reports.    1   2   3

# Following Oral Instructions

**DIRECTIONS:** Circle 1, 2, or 3 below to indicate your evaluation of each item.

| **Evaluation Scale:** | 1 = Not at all | 2 = To some extent | 3 = Successfully |
|---|---|---|---|

- In a group, each student draws a picture (but does not reveal it) and then clearly explains it to the other group members.    1   2   3

- As a speaker, the student uses effective verbal and nonverbal cues during his or her presentation.    1   2   3

- As a listener, the student uses common verbal cues to add to his or her understanding of a spoken message.    1   2   3

- As a listener, the student uses common nonverbal cues to add to his or her understanding of a spoken message.    1   2   3

- As a listener, the student limits distractions and focuses attention on the speaker.    1   2   3

- As a listener, he student takes effective notes using the guidelines on page 77 of the pupil's edition.    1   2   3

- As a listener, the student asks questions for clarification as needed.    1   2   3

- When asking questions, the student follows the guidelines on page 78 of the pupil's edition.    1   2   3

- Based on the speaker's explanation of his or her picture, the student attempts to draw the speaker's picture and then actively participates in a small group discussion of the differences and similarities of the group members' pictures.    1   2   3

- The student discusses the results of following oral instructions and thoughtfully evaluates the skills needed to more effectively follow oral instructions.    1   2   3

# Making a Documentary Video

**DIRECTIONS:** Circle 1, 2, or 3 below to indicate your evaluation of each item.

| **Evaluation Scale:** | 1 = Not at all | 2 = To some extent | 3 = Successfully |
|---|---|---|---|

- The student chooses and videotapes one or two appropriate television programs and notes the ways in which characters are portrayed.  1  2  3

- The student identifies any characters who fit common media stereotypes.  1  2  3

- The student evaluates these characters and rates them on a scale from stereotypical to realistic.  1  2  3

- The student's evaluation chart includes specific reasons and evidence for the student's evaluations.  1  2  3

- The student works collaboratively in a small group to plan and produce a documentary video.  1  2  3

- Group members make thoughtful decisions about the main ideas they want to convey to the audience.  1  2  3

- Group members choose an appropriate scene to analyze.  1  2  3

- The group creates useful storyboards of the chosen scene.  1  2  3

- Group members develop a script for the documentary.  1  2  3

- The narrator speaks clearly and loudly enough to be understood and matches his or her words to the scene shown during the taping of the documentary.  1  2  3

- The cameraperson uses the video equipment correctly, starting and stopping at the appropriate times and maintaining a steady, focused shot of the narrator and the scene being shown.  1  2  3

- The producer effectively cues the narrator and cameraperson and monitors the tape of the scene being shown in the documentary.  1  2  3

- Group members rehearse and revise the documentary as needed prior to videotaping.  1  2  3

- Group members evaluate and reshoot the documentary as needed after taping.  1  2  3

- Group members discuss and evaluate the finished documentary, noting how well the script fits the video images and how effectively the video medium conveys information.  1  2  3

for **CHAPTER FOUR: FOCUS ON VIEWING AND REPRESENTING** page 148 **RUBRIC**

# Designing and Creating a Book Cover

**DIRECTIONS:** Circle 1, 2, or 3 below to indicate your evaluation of each item.

| Evaluation Scale: | 1 = Not at all | 2 = To some extent | 3 = Successfully |
| --- | --- | --- | --- |

- The student can identify a variety of media that might be used to create a book cover.  1  2  3

- The student can identify the elements of a book cover.  1  2  3

- The student recognizes that a book cover may reveal information about characters, setting, or action or may represent an important emotion or idea in the book.  1  2  3

- The student understands the distinction between warm and cool colors and can identify the symbolic meaning of each type of color.  1  2  3

- The student analyzes a book cover based on the questions in the chart on page 150 of the pupil's edition.  1  2  3

- The student plans and creates an appropriate illustration for a new cover for a novel he or she has read.  1  2  3

- The student uses an appropriate medium to create the chosen illustration.  1  2  3

- The student makes effective color choices that convey emotions that fit the book.  1  2  3

- The student uses a font or fonts that fit the content of the chosen book.  1  2  3

- The cover lists the book's title and author and awards the book has won.  1  2  3

# Performing a Dramatic Reading

**DIRECTIONS:** Circle 1, 2, or 3 below to indicate your evaluation of each item.

> **Evaluation Scale:**    1 = Not at all    2 = To some extent    3 = Successfully

- The student chooses an appropriate and interesting passage for dramatic reading.     1    2    3
- The student edits the selection to eliminate content that might sound odd in a performance.     1    2    3
- The student adds information that listeners will need to understand what is happening in the scene.     1    2    3
- The student analyzes the characters and action in the scene.     1    2    3
- The student makes notes to guide his or her delivery of the dramatic reading.     1    2    3
- The student creates a script of the edited scene with performance notes in parentheses.     1    2    3
- The student rehearses the scene and evaluates the performance to make improvements.     1    2    3
- The student consistently uses voices that fit the characters in the scene and modulates his or her voice to fit emotions and actions during the scene.     1    2    3    1    2    3
- The student uses gestures appropriately to emphasize important parts of the scene, to show action, and to delineate characters.     1    2    3
- The student speaks loudly, clearly, and expressively.     1    2    3

# Giving and Listening to an Informative Speech

**DIRECTIONS:** Circle 1, 2, or 3 below to indicate your evaluation of each item.

| **Evaluation Scale:** | 1 = Not at all | 2 = To some extent | 3 = Successfully |
|---|---|---|---|

## Speaking

- The student considers how to adapt the information and word choice in the written report to the purpose, occasion, and audience of the speech.      1   2   3

- The student limits the speech to the main points and support or elaborations from his or her research report.      1   2   3

- The student uses a simple outline to guide the speech rather than reading the entire report.      1   2   3

- The student enunciates clearly and uses an effective rate of speech, volume, and vocal pitch to maintain audience understanding and interest.      1   2   3

- The speech is well rehearsed.      1   2   3

- If the student uses visuals, they add to audience understanding and include images or text large and clear enough to be seen from all parts of the room.      1   2   3

- The student explains any visuals used and faces the audience while doing so.      1   2   3

- If a video or audio segment is used, it adds to audience understanding and is properly cued up before the speech begins.      1   2   3

## Listening

- The student identifies a purpose for listening and makes predictions about the speech.      1   2   3

- The student focuses on the speaker and limits distractions.      1   2   3

- The student makes notes of the speaker's main points, listening for cues and summarizing as necessary.      1   2   3

- The student asks questions for clarification as needed.      1   2   3

ELEMENTS OF LANGUAGE | First Course | *Assessment Alternatives*

# Interpreting Graphics and Web Sites

**DIRECTIONS:** Circle 1, 2, or 3 below to indicate your evaluation of each item.

| **Evaluation Scale:** | 1 = Not at all | 2 = To some extent | 3 = Successfully |
|---|---|---|---|

- The student can identify four elements of graphics—the title, body, legend, and source.          1   2   3

- The student can list strategies for gathering information from maps.          1   2   3

- The student can list strategies for gathering information from tables.          1   2   3

- The student can list strategies for gathering information from line graphs.          1   2   3

- The student can list strategies for gathering information from time lines.          1   2   3

- The student answers the questions on page 196 of the pupil's edition correctly and can supply reasons for his or her answers.          1   2   3

- The student can identify features of a Web site, including an index and hyperlinks.          1   2   3

- The student develops strategies for searching a Web site for information.          1   2   3

# Analyzing an Editorial Cartoon

**DIRECTIONS:** Circle 1, 2, or 3 below to indicate your evaluation of each item.

| Evaluation Scale: | 1 = Not at all | 2 = To some extent | 3 = Successfully |
|---|---|---|---|

- The student chooses an appropriate editorial cartoon to analyze.  1  2  3

- The student identifies the issue addressed by the chosen editorial cartoon.  1  2  3

- The student identifies and analyzes the meaning of any symbols used in the chosen editorial cartoon.  1  2  3

- The student identifies any exaggeration or caricature used in the chosen editorial cartoon.  1  2  3

- The student analyzes the effect of any exaggeration or caricature on the meaning of the chosen editorial cartoon.  1  2  3

- The student identifies and analyzes the meaning of any analogies used in the chosen editorial cartoon.  1  2  3

- The student explains how the analogy helps to tell the story contained in the chosen editorial cartoon.  1  2  3

- The student identifies the cartoonist's opinion on the issue addressed in the chosen editorial cartoon.  1  2  3

- In a small group, the student discusses the similarities and differences among cartoons analyzed by group members, noting in particular the differences in topics, attitudes, and techniques in the various cartoons.  1  2  3

# Analyzing Visual Effects in Ads

**DIRECTIONS:** Circle 1, 2, or 3 below to indicate your evaluation of each item.

| ▶ **Evaluation Scale:** | 1 = Not at all | 2 = To some extent | 3 = Successfully |
|---|---|---|---|

- The student can identify differences between television and print advertisements.    1   2   3

- The student can identify types of visual effects used in advertisements and their effects on the message.    1   2   3

- The student chooses for analysis a print advertisement that uses at least one visual effect.    1   2   3

- The student chooses for analysis a television commercial that uses at least one visual effect.    1   2   3

- The student identifies the visual effects used in a print advertisement and analyzes how the effects influence or change the message.    1   2   3

- The student identifies the visual effects used in a television commercial and analyzes how the effects influence or change the message.    1   2   3

- The student compares the effectiveness of both ads, citing specific evidence for his or her evaluations.    1   2   3

# Introduction: *Choices* Activities

| **Evaluation Scale:** | 1 = Not at all | 2 = To some extent | 3 = Successfully |
|---|---|---|---|

## Writing

### 1. Exploring New Forms

- The student actively participates in class brainstorming.    1   2   3
- The student contributes ideas, handwriting, or artwork to the class poster.    1   2   3
- The student produces a piece of writing on the topic of his or her choice in a form he or she has not used previously.    1   2   3

## Speaking and Listening

### 2. Thinking About Listening

- The student actively listens to a speech, talk show, lecture, or news report.    1   2   3
- The student takes thorough notes on what he or she does before, during, and after listening.    1   2   3
- The student participates actively in a small group discussion about the group members' listening notes.    1   2   3
- The student actively contributes to an oral report that explains the group's conclusions about whether listening is a process.    1   2   3

## Reading

### 3. Dialogue with a Writer

- With a small group, the student chooses an appropriate text.    1   2   3
- The student reads the chosen text and makes notes in a reading log to work out any problems in understanding the text.    1   2   3
- The student compares his or her notes with the notes made by other students in the group and actively participates in a discussion about their shared and different reading experiences.    1   2   3

## Careers

### 4. Team Spirit

- In a small group, each student helps choose an appropriate topic for a piece of collaborative writing.    1   2   3
- The students equitably divide the tasks.    1   2   3
- Each student carefully performs his or her role— researching the topic, writing a first draft, or editing the draft to produce a final piece.    1   2   3
- The written product generally follows the conventions of grammar, usage, punctuation, and spelling, except when conventions are purposefully violated for effect (i.e., to make dialogue sound more natural).    1   2   3
- The written product follows the conventions of its form (film script, poetry, etc.).    1   2   3

**RUBRICS**

# Chapter One: *Choices* Activities

| **Evaluation Scale:** | 1 = Not at all | 2 = To some extent | 3 = Successfully |
|---|---|---|---|

## Crossing the Curriculum: Art

### 1. Create a World

- The student chooses an appropriate object to observe from a variety of perspectives.     1   2   3
- The student draws the object with careful attention to detail.     1   2   3
- The drawing creatively represents the object.     1   2   3

## Connecting Cultures

### 2. Once upon a Time

- The student identifies a favorite folktale or fairytale and conducts research to find examples of similar stories from at least two other cultures.     1   2   3
- The student identifies details from the tales that demonstrate their similarities and differences.     1   2   3
- The student presents findings aloud, speaking clearly and elaborating on ideas.     1   2   3

## Career: Journalism

### 3. On the Beat

- The student documents observations in a notebook for a week.     1   2   3
- The student identifies potential news stories that are interesting or unusual.     1   2   3
- The student compares observations and ideas with other students.     1   2   3
- The student actively contributes to a collaborative news story.     1   2   3

## Writing

### 4. Do You See Eye to Eye?

- With a partner, the student selects an appropriate object or event to observe.     1   2   3
- The students each write a brief description that includes details and careful observations.     1   2   3
- The descriptions are clear and relatively free of errors in spelling, grammar, usage, and mechanics     1   2   3
- The pair of students makes thoughtful comparisons between their two descriptions.     1   2   3
- The students notes details from both descriptions in discussing differences and similarities.     1   2   3

# Chapter One: *Choices* Activities *(continued)*

| **Evaluation Scale:** | 1 = Not at all | 2 = To some extent | 3 = Successfully |
|---|---|---|---|

## Drama

### 5. The Way I See It

- The student adapts his or her eyewitness account for dramatic interpretation.     1    2    3

- The student effectively organizes and directs other students, if applicable.     1    2    3

- The student speaks audibly, clearly, and expressively during the dramatization.     1    2    3

- The performance is smooth and well rehearsed.     1    2    3

# Chapter Two: *Choices* Activities

| Evaluation Scale: | 1 = Not at all | 2 = To some extent | 3 = Successfully |
|---|---|---|---|

## Art

### 1. That Covers It

- The student plans a cover for a how-to video based on the topic of his or her how-to essay.    1   2   3
- The video cover includes pictures, eye-catching headlines and titles, and a brief summary of the activity.    1   2   3
- The cover is creative, appealing, and neat.    1   2   3
- The summary is accurate and relatively free of errors in spelling, grammar, usage, and mechanics.    1   2   3

## Careers

### 2. What Goes On in Your Mind?

- In a small group, the student helps select an appropriate author and research the author's mailing address.    1   2   3
- The groups writes a letter to the author inquiring about his or her creative process.    1   2   3
- The letter is clear, polite, and relatively free of errors in spelling, grammar, usage, and mechanics.    1   2   3
- The group compares the response that he or she receives with responses received by other groups choosing this activity.    1   2   3

## Crossing the Curriculum: History

### 3. How It Was Done

- The student selects an appropriate historical activity to research.    1   2   3
- The student conducts research to learn about the process used in performing the activity.    1   2   3
- The student's flowchart clearly and accurately represents and explains the steps of the process.    1   2   3
- The student shares his or her findings with a small group of classmates.    1   2   3

# Chapter Two: *Choices* Activities *(continued)*

| **Evaluation Scale:** | 1 = Not at all | 2 = To some extent | 3 = Successfully |
|---|---|---|---|

## Investigation

### 4. What Makes It Tick?

- The student selects an appropriate mechanical device and conducts research to determine how the device works.  1  2  3
- The student clearly and thoroughly explains how the device works in either a technical drawing or a short essay.  1  2  3
- If the student chooses to create a technical drawing, the drawing is neat, clearly labeled, and easy to interpret.  1  2  3
- If the student chooses to write a short essay, the essay is well organized and relatively free of errors in spelling, grammar, usage, and mechanics.  1  2  3

## Creative Writing

### 5. How to Create a Snicker

- The student chooses an appropriate process to explain in the poem.  1  2  3
- The student creates humor by describing a silly process or by leaving out important steps in an ordinary process.  1  2  3
- The poem generally follows conventions of poetry, including organization into lines.  1  2  3
- The poem uses correct spelling, punctuation, and grammar except when conventions are purposefully violated to create an effect.  1  2  3

# Chapter Three: *Choices* Activities

▶ **Evaluation Scale:**     1 = Not at all     2 = To some extent     3 = Successfully

## Consumer Education

### 1. Do You Buy This?

- The student selects an appropriate product to evaluate and prewrites by listing the advantages and disadvantages of buying this particular product.　　1　2　3

- The student's review thoughtfully analyzes the advantages and disadvantages of buying the product and clearly states whether or not the student would choose to buy the product.　　1　2　3

- The review is clearly organized and uses generally correct spelling, punctuation, grammar, and usage.　　1　2　3

- The student collaborates with other students to create a useful database of product reviews.　　1　2　3

## Crossing the Curriculum: Art

### 2. Picture This

- The student creates a chart that clearly organizes and labels pictures of the advantages and disadvantages of his or her essay topic.　　1　2　3

- The pictures used in the chart clearly and creatively identify the advantages and disadvantages they represent.　　1　2　3

- The chart is neat, attractive, and eye-catching.　　1　2　3

## Speech

### 3. Hear Me Roar

- The student adapts his or her advantages and disadvantages essay into a speech.　　1　2　3

- The student persuasively supports one option over the other.　　1　2　3

- The student speaks clearly and audibly during the presentation.　　1　2　3

## Crossing the Curriculum: History

### 4. From the Past

- The student selects an appropriate event and reads two accounts or perspectives of the event.　　1　2　3

- The student prewrites by listing similarities and differences between the two accounts.　　1　2　3

- The student writes a paragraph that clearly and accurately explains the similarities and differences between the two accounts.　　1　2　3

- The paragraph generally follows the conventions of grammar, usage, spelling, and punctuation.　　1　2　3

# Chapter Three: *Choices* Activities *(continued)*

| **Evaluation Scale:** | 1 = Not at all | 2 = To some extent | 3 = Successfully |
|---|---|---|---|

### Careers

**5. The Results Are In**

- The student selects an appropriate work-related topic.  1  2  3
- The student researches the advantages and disadvantages of the topic by interviewing an adult about its potential effects.  1  2  3
- The student clearly and thoroughly presents the advantages and disadvantages of the topic in an oral report.  1  2  3
- The student speaks clearly and audibly during the oral report.  1  2  3

# Chapter Four: *Choices* Activities

| **Evaluation Scale:** | 1 = Not at all | 2 = To some extent | 3 = Successfully |
|---|---|---|---|

## Speaking

### 1. Lights, Camera, Action!

- The student considers purpose and audience as he or she plans a three-minute movie preview that showcases the same book for which the student prepared a book jacket.    1   2   3
- The preview includes information about the book's characters, setting, plot, and theme.    1   2   3
- As the preview narrator, the student presents a clear and interesting summary, speaking clearly and audibly throughout.    1   2   3
- If visuals are used, they are easy to see, fit the information presented in the preview, and are creatively drawn.    1   2   3

## Drama

### 2. Acting Out

- The student selects an appropriate poem to read aloud.    1   2   3
- The student demonstrates a clear understanding of the poem.    1   2   3
- The student dramatizes the poem by using gestures, pauses, and voice changes.    1   2   3
- The student speaks clearly and audibly during the presentation.    1   2   3

## Careers

### 3. Meet the Author

- The student identifies an author who fits assignment guidelines.    1   2   3
- The student researches the author's background and works.    1   2   3
- The student creates appropriate questions for the author and asks them.    1   2   3
- The student's journal entry records answers to his or her questions and reflects on the experience of talking with a published author.    1   2   3

## Crossing the Curriculum: Science

### 4. Experience Laboratory Life

- The student selects an appropriate science experiment and studies how the experiment works.    1   2   3
- The student develops a thoughtful and plausible hypothesis.    1   2   3
- The students conducts the experiment safely and correctly with an adult and carefully records the results.    1   2   3
- In a paragraph, the student thoughtfully analyzes why the hypothesis was or was not correct.    1   2   3
- The paragraph generally follows the conventions of grammar, usage, spelling, and punctuation.    1   2   3

# Chapter Five: *Choices* Activities

| Evaluation Scale: | 1 = Not at all | 2 = To some extent | 3 = Successfully |
|---|---|---|---|

## Careers

### 1. Get a Job!

| | | | |
|---|---|---|---|
| ▪ The student selects a career he or she might like to have and identifies a person with the chosen career. | 1 | 2 | 3 |
| ▪ The student writes a letter to the person identified asking for information on educational requirements and daily activities. | 1 | 2 | 3 |
| ▪ Using information from the response, the student writes an imaginative journal entry describing getting and performing the dream job. | 1 | 2 | 3 |
| ▪ The letter and journal entry are clear and relatively free of errors in spelling, grammar, usage, and mechanics. | 1 | 2 | 3 |

## Crossing the Curriculum: Social Studies

### 2. Where Did I Come From?

| | | | |
|---|---|---|---|
| ▪ The student researches his or her own family history. | 1 | 2 | 3 |
| ▪ The student creates a neat and easy-to-understand family tree with detailed information about some of the student's relatives. | 1 | 2 | 3 |
| ▪ The student writes a thoughtful and detailed memoir about an experience with a relative shown on the tree. | 1 | 2 | 3 |
| ▪ The memoir generally follows the conventions of grammar, usage, spelling, and punctuation. | 1 | 2 | 3 |

## Crossing the Curriculum: Math

### 3. Learning to Count

| | | | |
|---|---|---|---|
| ▪ The student researches either different methods of counting or the origin of mathematical symbols and ideas. | 1 | 2 | 3 |
| ▪ The student clearly and thoroughly explains his or her findings in an oral report. | 1 | 2 | 3 |
| ▪ The student speaks clearly and audibly during the report. | 1 | 2 | 3 |

## Drama

### 4. Let's Put on a Show

| | | | |
|---|---|---|---|
| ▪ The student adapts information from his or her research report into a puppet show for young children. | 1 | 2 | 3 |
| ▪ The student creates eye-catching puppets. | 1 | 2 | 3 |
| ▪ The student makes arrangements to perform the puppet show for a younger audience. | 1 | 2 | 3 |
| ▪ The student speaks clearly and audibly during the puppet show and maintains audience interest through lively actions and voices. | 1 | 2 | 3 |

# Chapter Five: *Choices* Activities *(continued)*

| Evaluation Scale: | 1 = Not at all | 2 = To some extent | 3 = Successfully |
|---|---|---|---|

## Connecting Cultures

**5. You Say Potato Pancake, I Say Latke**

- The student researches celebrations in other cultures.     1   2   3
- The student writes a report that thoughtfully compares and contrasts the celebrations of other cultures with his or her own culture's celebrations.     1   2   3
- The report is clear, well organized, and relatively free of errors in spelling, grammar, usage, and mechanics.     1   2   3

# Chapter Six: *Choices* Activities

| Evaluation Scale: | 1 = Not at all | 2 = To some extent | 3 = Successfully |
|---|---|---|---|

## Speech

### 1. Lay It on the Line

- The student selects an appropriate issue for a persuasive speech or considers how to adapt his or her persuasive essay.  1  2  3
- The reasons and evidence used in the speech appeal to the intended audience.  1  2  3
- The student presents the speech persuasively, speaking clearly and audibly and employing effective gestures and expressions.  1  2  3

## Careers

### 2. Tools of the Trade

- The student selects an appropriate career that requires skills of persuasion.  1  2  3
- The student researches how a person in that field uses persuasion.  1  2  3
- The student thoroughly and clearly explains his or her findings in a paragraph.  1  2  3
- The paragraph generally follows the conventions of grammar, usage, spelling, and punctuation.  1  2  3

## Art

### 3. See You in the Funny Papers

- The student creates a cartoon that clearly reflects his or her essay topic.  1  2  3
- The cartoon clearly expresses an opinion and is capable of being understood without reference to the essay.  1  2  3
- The cartoon demonstrates the student's creativity and attention to detail.  1  2  3

## Crossing the Curriculum: Social Studies

### 4. Time Traveling

- The student identifies an issue of interest to a person living in a time and place that the student has learned about in his or her social studies class.  1  2  3
- The student writes a persuasive letter that accurately and thoughtfully addresses the issue from the viewpoint of a person living in the culture studied.  1  2  3
- The letter is relatively free of errors in spelling, grammar, usage, and mechanics.  1  2  3

# Chapter Six: *Choices* Activities *(continued)*

| **Evaluation Scale:** | 1 = Not at all | 2 = To some extent | 3 = Successfully |
|---|---|---|---|

## Writing

### 5. What Is Your Problem?

- The student chooses an appropriate school or community issue and identifies the central problem.    1   2   3

- The student brainstorms and analyzes several possible solutions to the problem.    1   2   3

- The student writes an editorial clearly explaining the problem, proposing the best solution, and explaining why and how the solution will solve the problem.    1   2   3

- The editorial is relatively free of errors in spelling, grammar, usage, and mechanics.    1   2   3

# Chapter Seven: *Choices* Activities

| **Evaluation Scale:** | 1 = Not at all | 2 = To some extent | 3 = Successfully |
|---|---|---|---|

## Community Service

### 1. For a Good Cause

- The student selects an appropriate cause and identifies ways others can get involved in the cause.  1  2  3
- The student creates a persuasive poster, TV ad, or radio ad to encourage students and teachers to take a specific action to support the chosen cause.  1  2  3
- If the student creates a poster, it is neat and attractive and includes an eye-catching visual.  1  2  3
- If the student creates a TV or radio ad, the student speaks clearly and expressively and uses visuals or sound effects as appropriate.  1  2  3

## Crossing the Curriculum: Math

### 2. Charting the Course

- The student collaborates with two other students to collect twelve different print ads.  1  2  3
- The group works together to identify the main persuasive technique used in each ad.  1  2  3
- The group creates a paper or database record for each ad, describing the advertisement's content and listing the persuasive technique used.  1  2  3
- The group's pie chart accurately shows percentages based on the students' findings and is neat, clearly labeled, and easy to interpret.  1  2  3
- The group's presentation clearly explains which persuasive techniques are most commonly used in the ads the group studied.  1  2  3

## Crossing the Curriculum: Social Studies

### 3. History Hall of Fame

- The student chooses and researches an appropriate historical figure.  1  2  3
- The student plans and designs three or four accurate and persuasive print and TV ads.  1  2  3
- The student creates at least one of the ads. Print ads are neat, eye-catching, and easy to read. Television ads include appropriate visuals, and the student reads the ad copy clearly and expressively.  1  2  3

# Chapter Seven: *Choices* Activities *(continued)*

| **Evaluation Scale:** | 1 = Not at all | 2 = To some extent | 3 = Successfully |
|---|---|---|---|

## Careers

### 4. The Ad Game

- The student prepares a list of interview questions directly related to the career field chosen.     1   2   3

- The student arranges and conducts a phone interview with a member of the chosen field.     1   2   3

- The student writes a short report that clearly explains the information gained in the interview.     1   2   3

- The report generally follows conventions of grammar, usage, punctuation, and spelling.     1   2   3